1975
The Year That Transformed
BOLLYWOOD

Pratik Majumdar began his career in advertising, working in both India and London, before returning home to successfully run a family-owned homeopathy business.

A passionate cinephile, music enthusiast and published author of a collection of short stories, Pratik has amassed an impressive collection on Blu-rays, DVDs and vinyl records over the years. His articles on film have been published in the *Telegraph*, the *Daily Eye* and *Kolkata Konnect. 1975: The Year That Transformed Bollywood* is his first book on cinema.

Pratik lives in Kolkata with his parents and his wife, Bindiya. His daughter, Meghna, works in the United Kingdom.

1975

The Year That Transformed

BOLLYWOOD

Pratik Majumdar

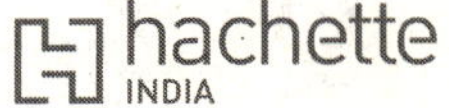

First published in 2025 by Hachette India
(Registered name: Hachette Book Publishing India Pvt. Ltd)
www.hachetteindia.com

1

ISBN 978-93-5731-763-4

Hachette Book Publishing India Pvt. Ltd
4th & 5th Floors, Corporate Centre
Plot No. 94, Sector 44, Gurugram – 122003, India

Typeset in Athelas 11/14
by Avishek Bhattacharya

Printed and bound in India
by Thomson Press India Ltd.

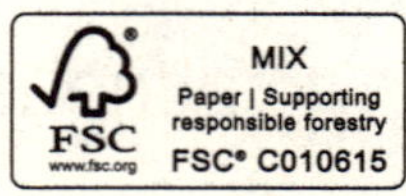

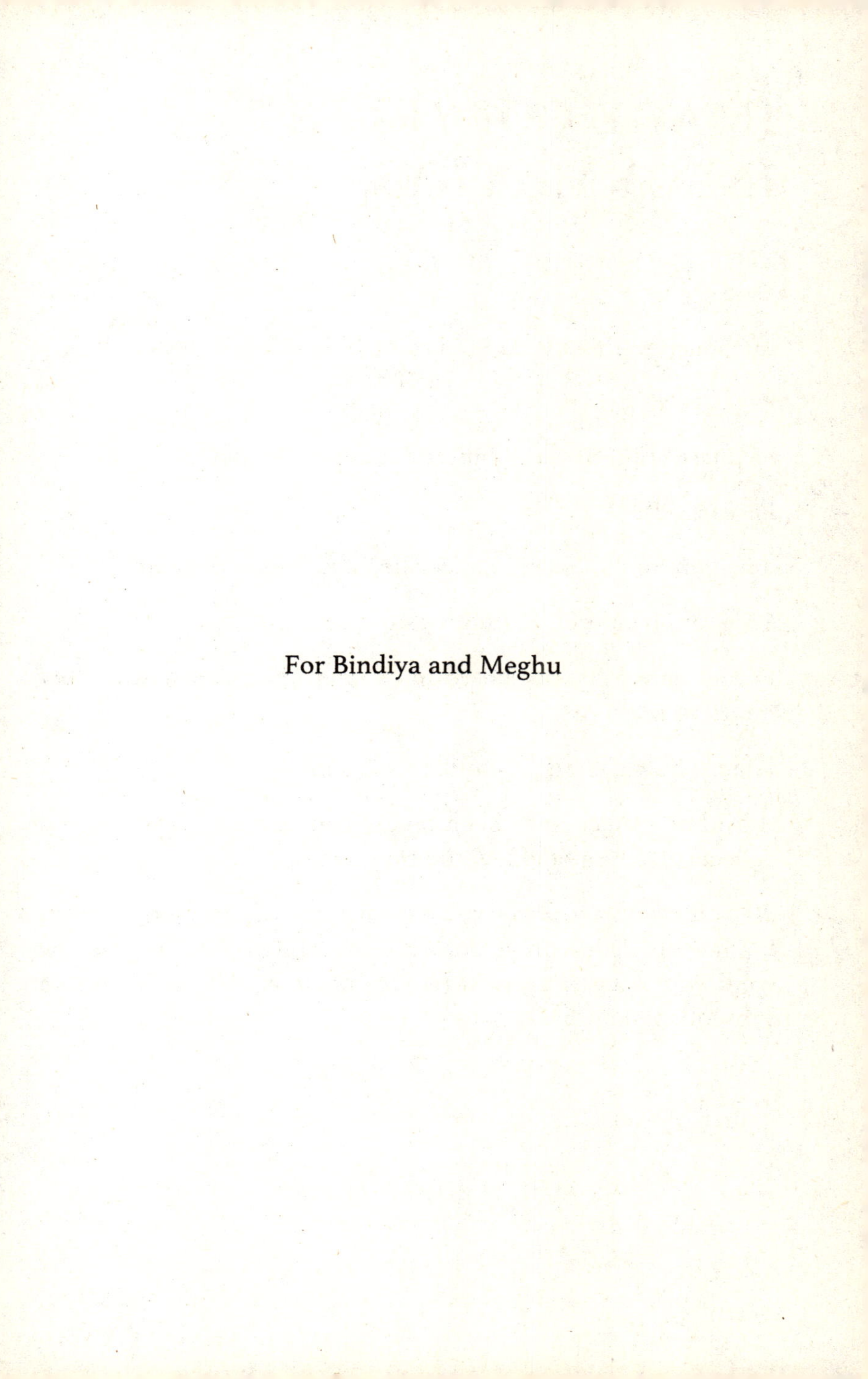

For Bindiya and Meghu

IMAGE COPYRIGHT INFORMATION

Page 9:

Introduction title block: Roman Amanov/Shutterstock.com

Pages 21, 22, 23:

Amanush stills: Shakti Films and Ashim Samanta

Pages 24, 25:

Amanush film booklet: Shakti Films and Ashim Samanta

Chapter opener: Bi.Std/Shutterstock.com

Film number clapper board in chapter opener: Kingwardobe/Shutterstock.com

Folio: Thomas Bethge/Shutterstock.com

All other images have been taken from the author's personal collection of film booklets and magazines.

A few images have unclear provenance and the last-known rights holder has been contacted, or been applied for. Any specific credit annotations brought to our notice will be carried out in subsequent editions.

CONTENTS

AUTHOR'S NOTE

If you're reading this, then most likely you've picked up this book. Thank you at the outset for that.

Welcome to a journey back in time – to the year 1975, a truly special moment in the world of Hindi cinema. As we look back fifty years later, I invite you to read these pages not just as a reader, but as a fellow movie lover – someone ready to step into the colourful, unforgettable world of Bollywood from that era.

The year 1975 was more than just another year at the movies. It was a turning point, a cultural moment when stories, songs, stars and the spirit of a nation converged on the silver screen. It was the year of *Sholay* and *Deewaar*, of *Chupke Chupke* and *Aandhi*, of *Jai Santoshi Maa* – films that didn't just entertain, but reflected the complexities, hopes and heartbeats of an entire generation. These were not just films; they were experiences that left an indelible mark on the Indian imagination.

In this book, I've tried to piece together that magic through a series of essays – each one revisiting a film, a film-maker or a phenomenon that defined the year. Whether you're a lifelong lover of Hindi cinema or someone discovering its vintage charm for the first time, I hope these reflections will open a window into an era where every line of dialogue echoed across time, every melody stirred the soul and every frame was steeped in passion.

So come, let's rewind the reels and immerse ourselves in a time when Bollywood was bold, beautiful and brimming with unforgettable stories. May this book help you not only understand 1975 – but feel it too.

INTRODUCTION

In the extensive history of Bollywood, few years shine as brightly as 1975, a pivotal time that proudly carved its niche in the Hindi film industry. Now, as we look back at the cinematic gems from this remarkable period fifty years later, the lasting impact of these films is simply irrefutable. This book, *1975: The Year That Transformed Bollywood*, honours the talent, variety and cultural significance of some of these works by delving into their creation and narratives as well as the ways in which they continue to resonate with audiences to date.

The films released in 1975 that this book covers were not merely celluloid tales but rather the product of a nation in transition. The Emergency had swept over India in 1975, resulting in social and political unrest that seeped into many film plots and characters. From riveting narratives of defiance and justice to heart-warming explorations of family, faith and romance, Bollywood in 1975 reflected the hopes, fears and complexities of a swiftly evolving society. This was a year rich in ideas, courageous storytelling and unforgettable artistry. Moreover, the icing on the cake was the fact that they were all filled with dollops and dollops of entertainment.

At the heart of this cinematic renaissance were the blockbusters that revolutionized the industry. *Sholay*, the unrivalled giant of Indian cinema, dazzled audiences with its grand production value, an enormous budget for its time, memorable characters and dialogues that became ingrained in everyday conversation. Likewise, Salim–Javed's meticulously crafted *Deewaar* encapsulated the frustrations of a generation by reimagining heroism through Amitabh Bachchan's legendary portrayal of the 'angry young man'. Yet 1975 offered more than just epic tales, with films like *Jai Santoshi Maa*, produced on a tight budget, emerging as cultural milestones of the time and demonstrating that faith and simplicity could shine as brightly as the biggest productions.

The year also ignited a wave of youthful vigour and creativity. The light-hearted musical *Khel Khel Mein* introduced a fun and engaging form of storytelling, while *Pratiggya* artfully combined comedy and action, much to the delight of viewers. Meanwhile, *Dharmatma*, inspired by *The Godfather*, showcased Bollywood's knack for taking international influences and weaving them into unique Indian narratives.

The year 1975 brought a remarkable cinematic spectrum by achieving a beautiful balance between commercial hits and artistic milestones. Alongside Amitabh Bachchan's 'angry young man' in *Deewaar* and *Sholay* co-existed the archetypal 'boy next door' Amol Palekar in *Chhoti Si Baat*. Gulzar crafted an impressive trio of films – *Khushboo*, *Aandhi* and *Mausam* – that examined intricate relationships with his customary poetic grace. Shyam Benegal's *Nishant* stood as a high watermark for parallel cinema, offering an unvarnished picture of oppression and defiance that resonated deeply amid political upheaval. Hrishikesh Mukherjee contributed with the delightful charm of *Chupke Chupke* and the poignant storytelling in *Mili*, skilfully blending humour and emotion.

The creation of these films is as intriguing as their narratives. From Ramesh Sippy's meticulous efforts to build the immersive world of *Sholay* to Gulzar's lyrical and screenwriting brilliance and Shyam Benegal's innovative storytelling techniques, 1975 was a time when film-makers carved bold new paths in the pursuit of excellence in cinema. The music from these films too remains timeless. Melodies from *Khel Khel Mein*, *Aandhi*, *Mausam* and *Khushboo* continue to echo through generations, proving that the songs of 1975 are as eternal as their stories.

The box office successes of these films were remarkable, with many setting new standards of achievement in cinema. Even more significantly, their cultural impact has persisted. Iconic lines from *Deewaar* are still recited with passion, and even the minutest characters from *Sholay* are etched into our memories; the enthusiastic devotion inspired by *Jai Santoshi Maa* continues to uplift spirits.

This book invites you to an exploration of these thirty unforgettable films. Each chapter focuses on the film's making, its reception during its release and its lasting influence. Together, these essays create a narrative that not only celebrates the cinematic excellence of 1975 but also highlights why this year remains foundational in Bollywood's growth.

The year 1975 was more than just a calendar year – it was a movement. Join us as we delve into its legacy and rediscover the magic that shaped the heart of Bollywood.

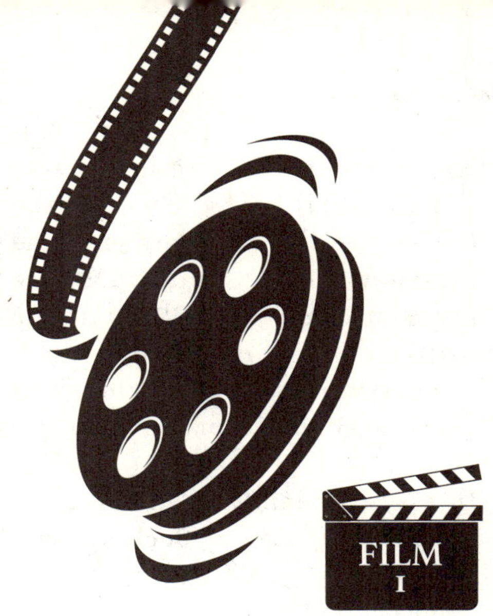

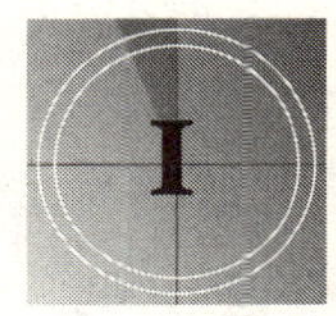

AANDHI: A CINEMATIC MASTERPIECE ENVELOPED IN CONTROVERSY

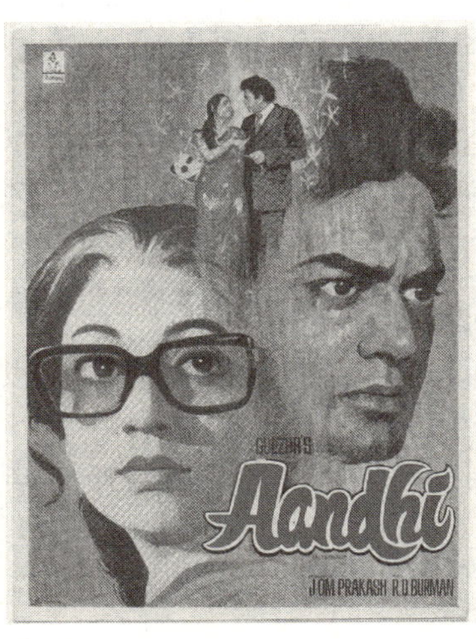

Gulzar's *Aandhi* holds a special place in Indian cinema not only for its touching narrative but also for the political uproar it inadvertently sparked a few weeks after its release. Crafted by Bhushan Banmali, Kamleshwar and Gulzar himself, the film serves as a deeply personal journey involving love, ambition and the repercussions of individual choices. However, its debut was overshadowed

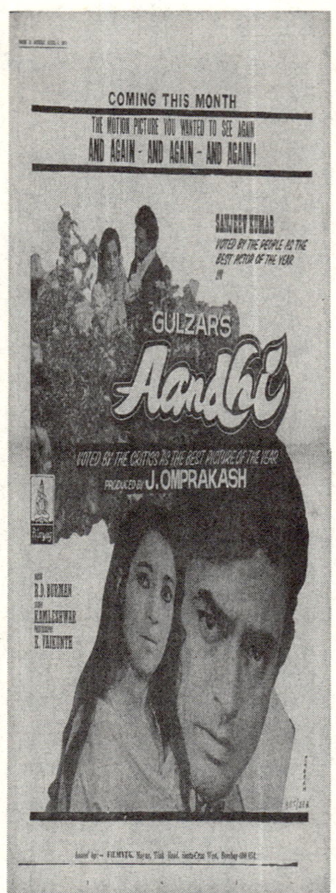

by controversy, culminating in a ban during the Emergency (1975–1977) enforced by the then-prime minister Indira Gandhi. Despite the controversy, the film's artistic brilliance remains undiminished, cementing its status as a cherished classic in Hindi cinema.

In essence, *Aandhi* is the story of Aarti Devi (played by Suchitra Sen), an ambitious and accomplished politician, and her estranged husband, J.K. (played by Sanjeev Kumar), a hotel owner. The film unfolds as a delicate study of a marriage strained by political ambition, personal goals and the expectations that come with public life. Flashbacks reveal Aarti and J.K.'s passionate love story, ultimately leading to their separation as Aarti chooses to focus on her political career over her personal life. Years later, fate reunites them, prompting the film's audience to question whether their love can endure the trials of time, ambition and regret.

Gulzar, celebrated for his sensitive portrayal of human relationships, skilfully navigates the narrative with subtlety and emotional richness. The dialogues sparkle with poetic beauty and steer clear of melodrama, instead utilizing the subdued yet potent performances of its lead actors.

Suchitra Sen's interpretation of Aarti Devi stands out as one of the most unforgettable performances in Hindi cinema. Her dignified presence, expressive gaze and nuanced acting vividly encapsulate Aarti's inner struggles. She embodies the complexity of a woman in power, caught between love and responsibility, through her graceful performance and quiet resilience.

Sanjeev Kumar, as J.K., enhances Sen's portrayal with his understated acting. He embodies a man who once deeply loved Aarti but grapples with his secondary status in her life. His heartache, disillusionment and affection for Aarti render him an empathetic figure. Together, their chemistry is electric yet heartbreakingly controlled, making their moments of reunion and nostalgia all the more poignant.

No discussion of *Aandhi* would be complete without acknowledging its exceptional music, created by Rahul Dev (R.D.) Burman, with lyrics by Gulzar. The soundtrack ranks among the most hauntingly beautiful in Hindi cinema. '*Tere Bina Zindagi Se Koi*', sung by Lata Mangeshkar and Kishore Kumar, captures the poignant emotions of loss and longing. This song continues to resonate with audiences, evoking the bittersweet ache of unfulfilled love. '*Tum Aa Gaye Ho Noor Aa Gaya Hai*', a melody infused with the warmth of rekindled love, stands out as one of R.D. Burman's most cherished compositions. '*Iss Mod Se Jaate Hain*' serves as another masterpiece that metaphorically reflects life's dilemmas and choices, echoing the film's core themes of separation and reunion.

The songs in *Aandhi* not just serve as musical breaks but also amplify the narrative's emotional weight. Even fifty years later, these songs remain indelibly etched in the minds of Hindi film

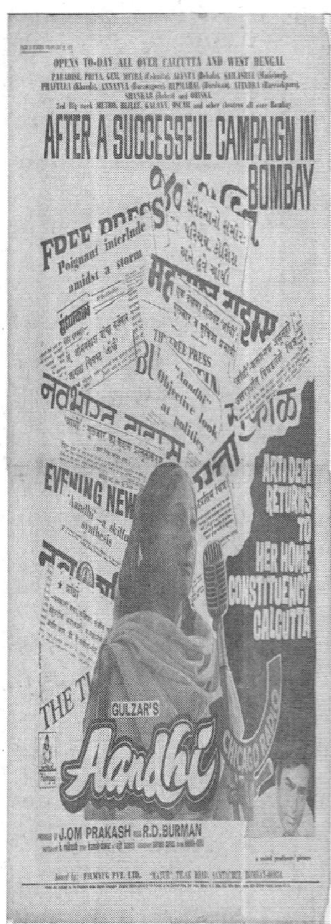

audiences. *Aandhi* likely represents the pinnacle of the Gulzar–R.D. Burman collaboration, which also gave us many other memorable film soundtracks such as *Khushboo*, *Kinara*, *Parichay*, *Ghar* and *Ijaazat*.

Despite its deeply romantic and emotional core, *Aandhi* found itself entangled in political controversy when it was released. The character of Aarti Devi, portrayed as a strong and ambitious female politician, bore a striking resemblance to Indira Gandhi, the then-prime minister of India. This connection was further emphasized by Sen's clothing and mannerisms and similarities with Indira Gandhi's public persona. Gulzar clearly said that Mrs Gandhi was merely an inspiration and the film did not follow her personal life. Tarkeshwari Sinha was also cited as another inspiration for the character. Tarkeshwari Sinha was an Indian politician who took part in the Quit India Movement. After Independence, she became the first female deputy finance minister (from 1958 to 1964) in the Union cabinet led by the then-prime minister Jawaharlal Nehru.

The political landscape during this period was highly volatile. After the Emergency was declared on 25 June 1975, severe censorship was imposed on films, the press and political discussions. The government alleged that *Aandhi* (in its twenty-third week of successful run) was a thinly veiled critique of Indira Gandhi, despite Gulzar's insistence that the film did not mirror her life. This uproar resulted in a ban on public screenings during the Emergency. After several edits and the addition of some new scenes (including one mandated by the administration), as well as the end of the Emergency and arrival of a new government, *Aandhi* was eventually released again and also made its TV premiere on the state-run channel *Doordarshan* in 1977.

Nonetheless, *Aandhi* has solidified its position as one of the most significant films in Indian cinema. Its examination of gender dynamics, personal sacrifices and the emotional toll of ambition has ensured its continued relevance. Unlike many political dramas of its time, *Aandhi* refrains from taking a decisive stance; instead, it invites audiences to interpret the story through their own perspectives.

Moreover, the controversy surrounding the film unintentionally elevated it to legendary status. Over the years, it has been reassessed not only as a political commentary but also as a profoundly moving love story. The film also opened doors for more nuanced portrayals of women in power within Indian cinema through their representation as complex figures rather than mere caricatures.

Aandhi serves as a testament to Gulzar's storytelling prowess, his ability to depict human emotions with finesse and his nuanced understanding of relationships. The film's ban during the Emergency remains a blemish on the history of Indian censorship, yet it simultaneously highlights the power of cinema to challenge authority, often without intent. Today *Aandhi* is celebrated for the artistry it embodies – brilliant performances, timeless melodies and a narrative that continues to captivate audiences. It stands as a landmark in Hindi cinema, proving that genuine art can transcend political upheaval and remain eternally significant.

CAST: Sanjeev Kumar, Suchitra Sen, Om Shivpuri, A.K. Hangal, Om Prakash
OTHER CREDITS: Directed by Gulzar.
Written by Bhushan Banmali, Kamleshwar, Gulzar.
Music by R.D. Burman.
RELEASE DATE: 14 February 1975
BOX OFFICE RESULT: Hit
RUNNING TIME: 2 Hours 13 Mins
TRIVIA: Producer J. Om Prakash wanted to sign Suchitra Sen and Sanjeev Kumar for a thriller film set inside a hospital, which was written by Sachin Bhowmik. Gulzar, however, wasn't very enthused by the premise and suggested making a film on a marriage broken by personal ambition and divided by egos. J. Om Prakash loved the idea and asked Gulzar to begin working on the script.

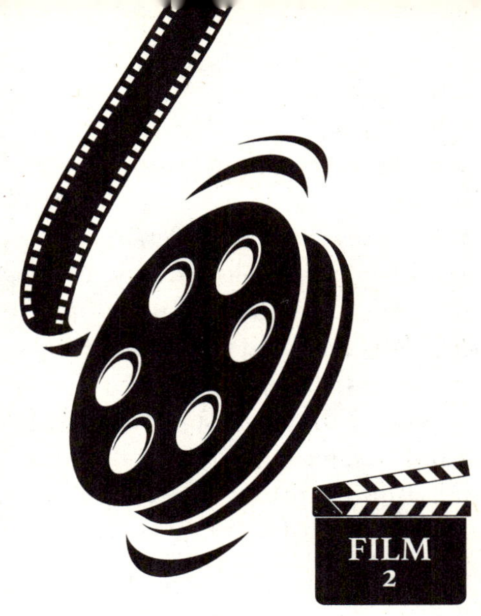

SHAKTI SAMANTA'S *AMANUSH*: A FILM THAT SHOWED WHAT BOLLYWOOD WAS MISSING

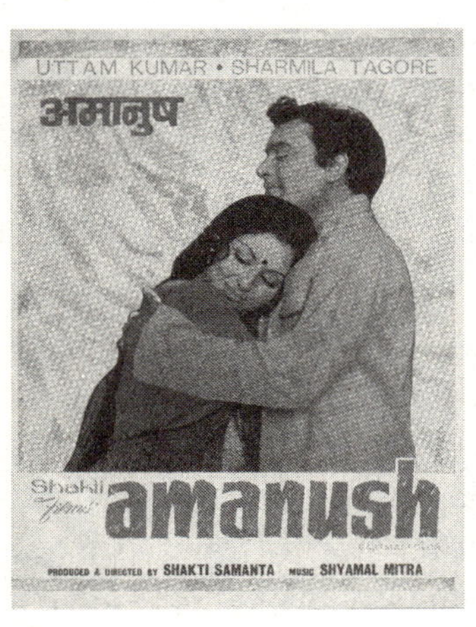

Shakti Samanta's *Amanush* is a film that beautifully bridges the worlds of Bollywood and Bengali cinema, reflecting the unique characteristics of both while delivering a stirring tale of redemption. It stands out not just as a captivating film but also as a platform showcasing the extraordinary yet largely underutilized talent of Uttam Kumar in Hindi films. Although he was the reigning star of Bengali cinema, his initial foray into Bollywood had been brief and largely unsuccessful. His Hindi film debut with *Chhoti Si Mulaqat* (1967), a remake of his Bengali hit *Agni Pariksha* (1954), fell flat at the box office and hit him hard financially. Feeling disillusioned, he retreated from Bollywood and went back to Kolkata (then Calcutta), where he continued to shine in Bengali cinema. However, when the talented Shakti Samanta – a director known for merging mainstream Bollywood storytelling with artistic flavours – offered him *Amanush*, a bilingual venture filmed in both Bengali and Hindi, it provided Uttam Kumar a chance to reintroduce himself to Hindi audiences and remind them of the remarkable actor they had overlooked.

Based on Shaktipada Rajguru's novel *Naya Basat*, *Amanush* tells the emotional story of Madhusudan Roy Chowdhury, a young man from a wealthy zamindar family, whose life spirals downward due to his own innocence and the scheming people around him. Wrongfully accused of a crime, Madhusudan is imprisoned and becomes a shattered soul who turns to alcohol in his downfall. Once a privileged heir, he now finds himself a despised outcast, even rejected by his beloved Lekha, portrayed by Sharmila Tagore. Madhusudan's tragic fall is orchestrated by the deceitful Maheem Ghoshal, played with chilling menace by Utpal Dutt. However, hope for Madhusudan arrives in the form of an idealistic police officer, played by Anil Chatterjee, who is able to look past Madhusudan's arrogance and despair and takes it upon himself to help him reclaim his dignity, wealth and love.

The film's storyline follows a familiar Bollywood path of decline and revival; yet what sets *Amanush* apart from standard melodrama is its profound emotional impact and Uttam Kumar's exceptional performance. The role of Madhusudan suited

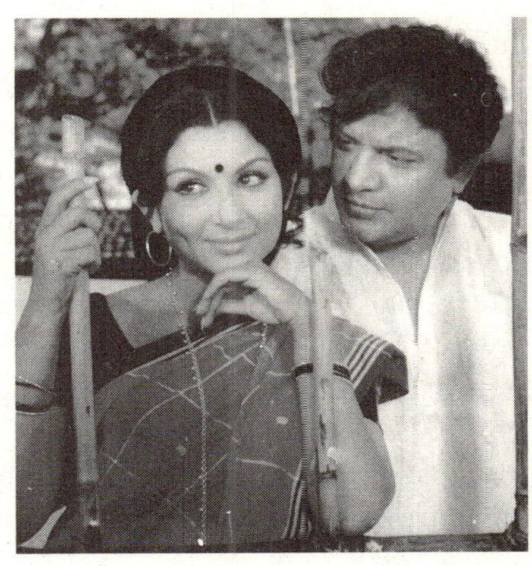

him perfectly, allowing him to convey a wide emotional range – from the dignified heir to the dishevelled drunkard and ultimately to the redeemed man who finds justice and wins back his self-respect. His ability to internalize suffering and communicate it through subtle details rather than overt dramatics makes his portrayal immensely captivating. While Bollywood was then dominated by over-the-top heroes, Uttam Kumar's acting style was grounded in realism. In *Amanush*, he does not depict Madhusudan as a mere tragic figure but as a man whose pain is deeply felt by the viewer, with his silence often saying more than his words.

One of the film's standout features is its villain, Maheem Ghoshal, played with aplomb by Utpal Dutt. Known for his diverse range, Dutt delivered one of his most evil performances in this movie. His Maheem doesn't rely on brute strength; he is shrewd, manipulative and utterly despicable in his calculated malice. The stark contrast between Madhusudan's raw emotional agony and Maheem's chilling machinations creates gripping tension throughout the film. *Amanush* is just as much a tale of power and deceit as it is of personal redemption, raising the viewing experience beyond a simple revenge narrative.

Sharmila Tagore's Lekha brings a certain depth to the film,

despite her role being largely supportive compared to the male leads. She serves as a representation of the social judgement that Madhusudan endures, with her rejection of him symbolizing how society often turns its back on those who have fallen. Her eventual return is more than a mere rekindling of love; it's an acknowledgement of the injustice he faced. While she delivers a formidable performance, her character arc feels somewhat predictable due to the clichéd trope of the estranged lover who returns after the hero regains his dignity.

Musically, *Amanush* flourishes thanks to Shyamal Mitra's enchanting compositions that embellish the film. Songs such as *'Na Puchho Koi Humein'*, *'Kal Ke Apne Na Jaane'* and *'Nadiya*

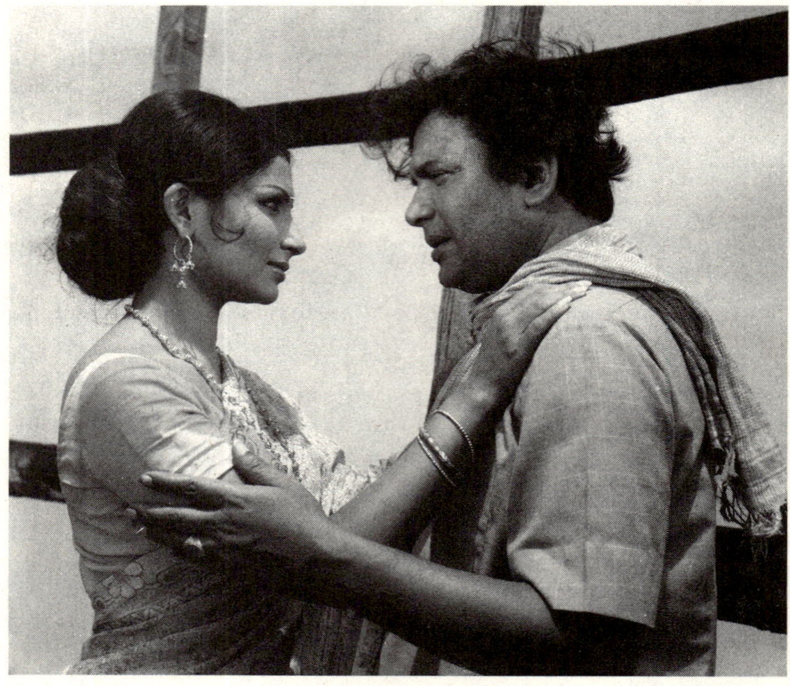

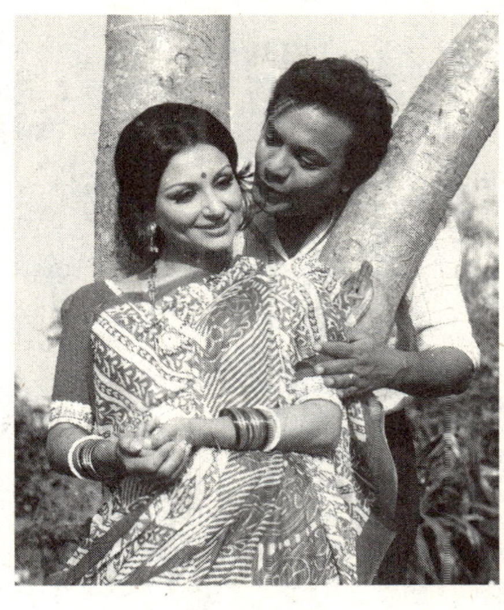

Mein Lehrein Naache' beautifully encapsulate the film's melancholic mood. However, the standout track is *'Dil Aisa Kisi Ne Mera Toda'*, sung by Kishore Kumar, which became one of the most unforgettable heartbreak songs in Bollywood history. This song profoundly expresses Madhusudan's pain and isolation and enhances its emotional weight within the film. The soundtrack, much like the film, demonstrates a balance between Bollywood's grand musical style and the more introspective, poetic elements typical of Bengali cinema.

Visually, *Amanush* shines under Shakti Samanta's confident direction that enables him to craft an aesthetically pleasing and emotionally resonant film. The film's setting, especially the rural landscapes and riverbanks of the Sunderbans, contributes to its immersive experience. There's an undeniable Bengali flavour running throughout the film, exemplified by its atmospheric cinematography, melancholic tone and a deep-seated exploration of themes like honour and redemption. Samanta's choice to create *Amanush* as a bilingual endeavour was a clever move, allowing both Bengali and Hindi audiences to engage with the story in a way that felt authentic to their cultural contexts. Although the film has a distinctly Bengali undertone, the emotional quotient of the film resonated with cinemagoers all over India.

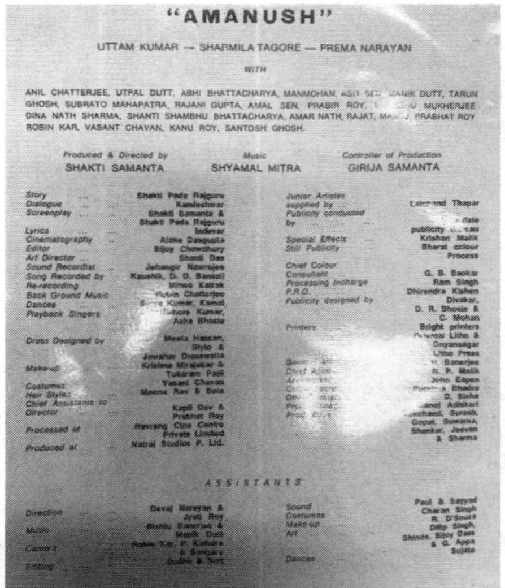

Despite its many strengths, *Amanush* is not without its shortcomings. At times, the narrative feels drawn out, and certain scenes seem to linger longer than they should. The melodramatic elements, particularly in the latter half, occasionally border on being excessive and just about manage to remain within the acceptable bounds of 1970s' Bollywood storytelling. Furthermore, while Uttam Kumar's performance is captivating, the film does not delve deeply enough into the psychological complexities of his character's trauma. His transformation from a hopeless drunkard to a reformed man is depicted more as a dramatic shift rather than through gradual personal growth, which slightly undermines the emotional arc of his redemption.

The film's popularity solidified Shakti Samanta's standing as a director skilled at telling emotionally engaging stories, and it continues to be one of the standout films from its era. A box office hit, *Amanush* is a tale of second chances both for its main character and, in a sense, for Uttam Kumar himself in the realm of Bollywood. Even if Hindi cinema didn't completely embrace his genius, *Amanush* ensured that his influence would be remembered, no matter how fleeting his time in the industry was.

Director Ashim Samanta, who is also the son of Shakti Samanta, recalls: *Amanush* was perhaps the first movie that was made simultaneously in Hindi and Bengali. In the Sunderbans those days, nothing was available, not even a needle. Here we created accommodation for a unit of one hundred and fifty people, a huge kitchen, a dining hall, a recreation room and the works. The entire place was powered by three huge generators.

After shooting in the Sunderbans for forty days, the unit returned to Mumbai. The sets were recreated in the studios where the indoors were shot.

CAST: Uttam Kumar, Sharmila Tagore, Utpal Dutt, Prema Narayan, Anil Chatterjee
OTHER CREDITS: Directed by Shakti Samanta. Music by Shyamal Mitra.
RELEASE DATE: 21 March 1975 (In Hindi)
BOX OFFICE RESULT: Hit
RUNNING TIME: 2 Hours 33 Mins
TRIVIA: When *Amanush* was being planned, Rajesh Khanna, a regular in Shakti Samanta's films, expressed his desire to act in the Hindi version alongside Uttam's Bengali version. Shakti Samanta was, however, sure about wanting Uttam Kumar to do the role in both versions, much to Khanna's disappointment.

With inputs from Ashim Samanta

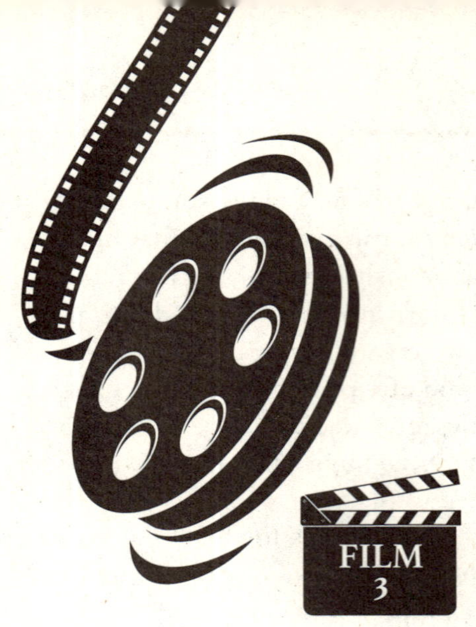

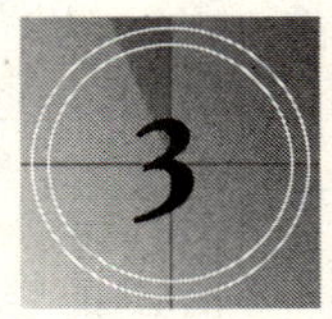

CHARANDAS CHOR: A SATIRICAL FOLK FABLE REIMAGINED FOR THE SILVER SCREEN

Shyam Benegal's *Charandas Chor* is a cinematic paradox; it is a film that is simple yet simultaneously layered with profound satire. Based on Habib Tanvir's celebrated play of the same name, which itself was adapted from a Rajasthani folk tale, the film traverses the fine line between fable and philosophy. Though it is meant to be a light-hearted children's film, it reveals a deeper, biting critique of society's hypocrisy, the corruptive nature of power and the cost of absolutism in a morally fluid world.

Habib Tanvir's play, which had already captivated Indian theatre audiences with its folk storytelling and biting satire, serves as the cultural and thematic foundation for Benegal's film. Rooted in the traditional *nautanki* performance style, Tanvir's version combined music, earthy humour and incisive social commentary. Benegal retained the essence of this form while translating it into the cinematic medium by using the folk narrative structure to hold a mirror up to Indian society and its institutions.

The protagonist, Charandas, is a thief; however, unlike his stereotypical counterparts, he is governed by a moral code that makes him paradoxically 'honest'. His integrity lies not in obedience to law but in his unflinching adherence to the promises he makes to his guru. This oxymoronic construct of a thief bound by personal ethics allows Benegal to explore the absurdities and contradictions within constructs of honesty, power and virtue.

Although Charandas's four promises – never to lie, never to lead a procession in his name, never to eat from a golden plate and never to marry a princess – are seemingly arbitrary and improbable, they become the narrative mechanisms that steer his journey towards his inevitable doom. Each promise is symbolic, indicating a refusal to participate in the traditional markers of power and success. Ironically, his death is not caused by his crimes but by his unwavering commitment to these promises. This ending serves as a scathing commentary on a society where integrity is not only undervalued but also fatal.

Benegal uses humour and irony to devastating effect. The satire isn't loud or didactic, but rather subtle and cumulative. The royal court that offers Charandas a golden plate and a princess, played by Smita Patil, in marriage is not doing so out of admiration but as a means of co-opting dissent – a familiar practice in any power structure threatened by non-conformity. Charandas's refusal is not perceived as moral strength but as insanity, and his death appears both comical and tragic through a farce that ends in martyrdom.

In this way, *Charandas Chor* critiques not just the ruling elite but also the very nature of social compromise. It exposes the societal machinery that punishes those who refuse to conform and celebrates the ones who adapt and manipulate. It is a direct satire of how the political, religious and cultural systems coerce individuals to trade their principles for survival or success.

Benegal's direction is deceptively simple. He uses the trappings of folk theatre, such as minimalistic sets, music and open acting, to retain the flavour of the original play while also leveraging the camera to enhance its emotional and political depth. The framing is theatrical yet intimate, the songs are narrative and not ornamental, and the humour is breezy but barbed.

The film also marked the screen debut of Smita Patil, who would go on to become one of India's most respected actresses. Though her role was limited, her presence hinted at the naturalistic screen presence she would go on to master. The rest of the cast included villagers and local performers, thereby bringing an authenticity to the film's folkloric charm.

Following the intense and politically charged *Nishant*, *Charandas Chor* may have seemed like a tonal detour for Benegal. Nonetheless, in hindsight, it demonstrates his versatility and commitment to telling stories rooted in India's diverse narrative traditions while never losing sight of contemporary relevance. It is this duality of the timelessness of folklore and urgency of social critique that gives the film its enduring power.

Charandas Chor is a masterclass in how satire can be used in cinema to critique society without losing the enjoyment of storytelling. It masquerades as a children's tale but is filled with deep philosophical insight and political bite. It mocks the powerful, elevates the outcast and suggests that sometimes, in a corrupt world, it is not crime that leads to destruction but unwavering honesty.

CAST: Lalu Ram, Smita Patil, Sadhu Meher, Habib Tanvir, Sunder
OTHER CREDITS: Directed by Shyam Benegal. Music by Nandkishore Mittal.
RELEASE DATE: 1975
BOX OFFICE RESULT: Average
RUNNING TIME: 2 Hours 36 Mins
TRIVIA: Shyam Benegal's use of Brechtian alienation, a theatrical technique started by Bertolt Brecht (hence the name), in *Charandas Chor* was one of his first trysts with this method as well as the first time it was used in Indian cinema. The movie compels its audience to use their intellect to decide the morality of the character rather than 'being told'. Benegal also changed the ending of the film from the play by Habib Tanvir. Whilst the protagonist dies in both the play and the film, Benegal adds an interesting and humorous epilogue wherein after his death, Charandas steals the bull belonging to Yamraj – the Hindu deity of death and the afterlife – and continues along his merry way.

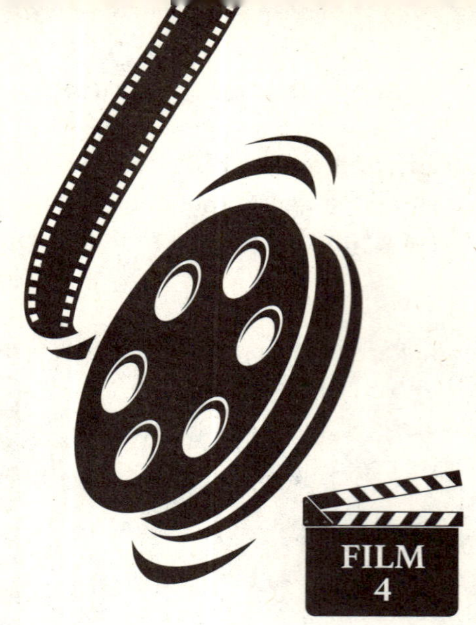

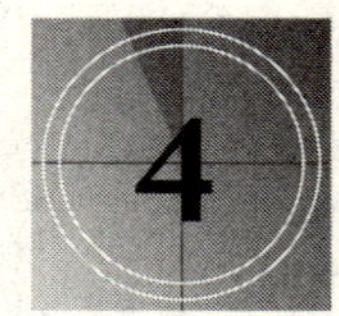

CHHOTI SI BAAT: A WHOLESOME ROMANTIC COMEDY

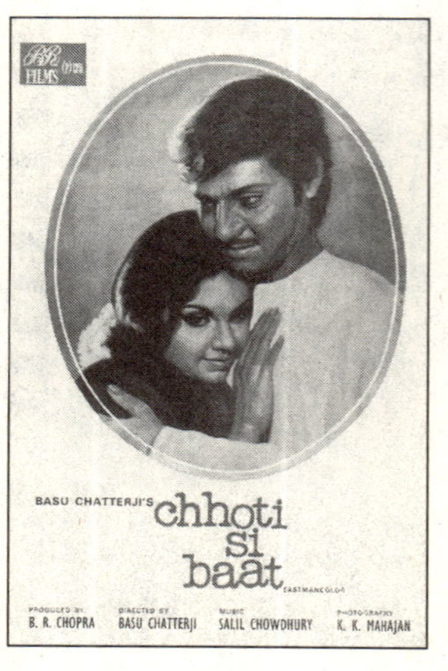

Basu Chatterjee's *Chhoti Si Baat* is a cherished gem of Indian cinema that is loved even today for its charming simplicity, wit and relatable storytelling. This film is the epitome of Chatterjee's incredible knack for capturing those little moments of life and transforming them into a delightful cinematic experience. A tender romantic comedy inspired by the 1960 British film *School for Scoundrels*, *Chhoti Si Baat* remains a beloved classic that resonates with audiences of all ages.

The narrative revolves around Arun Pradeep (portrayed by Amol Palekar), a timid and humble man who finds himself smitten with Prabha (Vidya Sinha), a colleague he admires. However, Arun's lack of self-confidence and his struggle to express his feelings lead to a series of funny yet heartrending adventures. Enter Colonel Julius Nagendranath Wilfred Singh (Ashok Kumar), an eccentric yet sagely character who becomes Arun's mentor, guiding him on the path to developing confidence and winning Prabha's heart. The story blends humour, romance and valuable life lessons to provide a refreshing alternative to the melodrama that was common in films of that era.

One of the film's most enchanting qualities is its down-to-earth nature. Basu Chatterjee, a pioneer of middle-of-the-road cinema, steered clear of lavish sets, excessive plot twists and over-the-top characters. Instead, he focused on the everyday lives of middle-class individuals with his authentic depictions of their struggles, dreams and emotions. The film's themes of love, uncertainty and hesitation strike a universal chord, making it an enduring tale. *Chhoti Si Baat* is also known for its cameos by three major Bollywood stars of the era – Dharmendra, Hema Malini and Amitabh Bachchan – who show up as themselves, much to the delight and surprise of viewers.

Amol Palekar's portrayal of Arun Pradeep can be considered one of the film's highlights. His understated performance captures the essence of a shy and endearing man, allowing audiences to connect with and root for Arun. Vidya Sinha, as Prabha, radiates charisma and poise in her embodiment of the girl-next-door. The film's overall charm is enhanced by the genuine and electrifying chemistry between the lead pair. Ashok Kumar, as the quirky Colonel, commands attention through his remarkable comic timing and fatherly wisdom. His unique way of guiding Arun to win Prabha's affection results in some of the film's most memorable moments.

The soundtrack of *Chhoti Si Baat* crafted by Salil Chowdhury significantly enhances its enduring appeal. Melodic songs like '*Na Jaane Kyon*' and '*Jaaneman Jaaneman*' are not only delightful but integral to the story by enriching the narrative's emotional depth. The lyrics, penned by Yogesh, echo the film's overall simplicity by effortlessly combining poetry with simplicity.

What truly makes *Chhoti Si Baat* timeless are its universally relatable themes. The film reminds us that true love isn't about grand gestures but about real feelings, commitment and personal growth. Arun's journey from a shy admirer to a confident suitor serves as a metaphor for self-discovery.

Over the past fifty years, *Chhoti Si Baat* has inspired countless film-makers and continues to set a high standard for romantic comedies in Bollywood. Its influence can be seen in the works of contemporary directors striving to capture the simplicity and authenticity that Chatterjee mastered. The film's legacy teaches us that powerful storytelling doesn't require hefty budgets or star-studded casts; instead, it can thrive on a good story showcasing a profound understanding of human emotions conveyed with genuineness and humour.

As we celebrate the golden journey of *Chhoti Si Baat*, it's evident that the film's charm lies in its ability to make us laugh, reflect and value the importance of small moments. In today's fast-paced, high-energy cinema world, *Chhoti Si Baat* serves as a gentle reminder of the beauty found in simplicity.

CAST: Amol Palekar, Vidya Sinha, Ashok Kumar, Asrani (Dharmendra, Hema Malini, Amitabh Bachchan in guest appearances)
OTHER CREDITS: Directed by Basu Chatterjee. Music by Salil Chowdhury.
RELEASE DATE: 9 January 1975
BOX OFFICE RESULT: Hit
RUNNING TIME: 2 Hours 03 Mins
TRIVIA: When initially released, the film posters featured the super-hit duo Dharmendra and Hema Malini (they appear in one song, '*Jaaneman Jaaneman*', in the film) more prominently than the lead pair – Amol Palekar and Vidya Sinha – who were still relatively lesser-known despite the success of their earlier film, *Rajnigandha*.

The film was produced by Bollywood veteran B.R. Chopra, who was also simultaneously producing *Zameer*, directed by his son Ravi Chopra. A banner for *Zameer* features prominently at a bus stop in a few scenes from *Chhoti Si Baat*. Amitabh Bachchan, who was the leading star of *Zameer*, also makes a guest appearance as himself in his *Zameer* get-up.

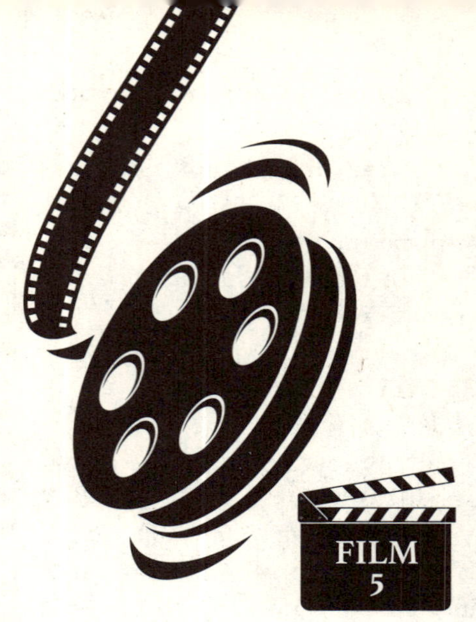

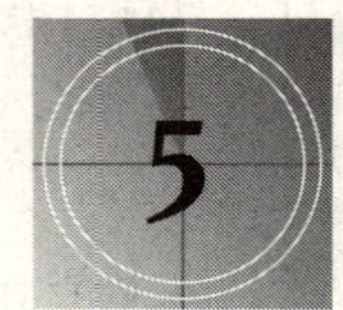

BRIJ SADANAH'S *CHORI MERA KAAM*: AN ENTERTAINING TALE OF CRIME, COMEDY AND CHAOS

Brij Sadanah's *Chori Mera Kaam* is a vibrant example from Bollywood's golden era for commercial cinema, characterized by films that masterfully combined crime, comedy, drama and music into a captivating viewing experience. Following the remarkable triumph of *Victoria No. 203* (1972), Brij once again demonstrated his talent for creating a 'masala' entertainer rich with excitement, emotion and intrigue. Despite its reliance on coincidences and exaggerated events, the film continues to be popular with Bollywood fans owing to its humour and enjoyable narrative.

Chori Mera Kaam is a playful yet adventurous story revolving around Bhola (Shashi Kapoor) and Sharmili (Zeenat Aman), two small-time thieves who inadvertently discover an unpublished

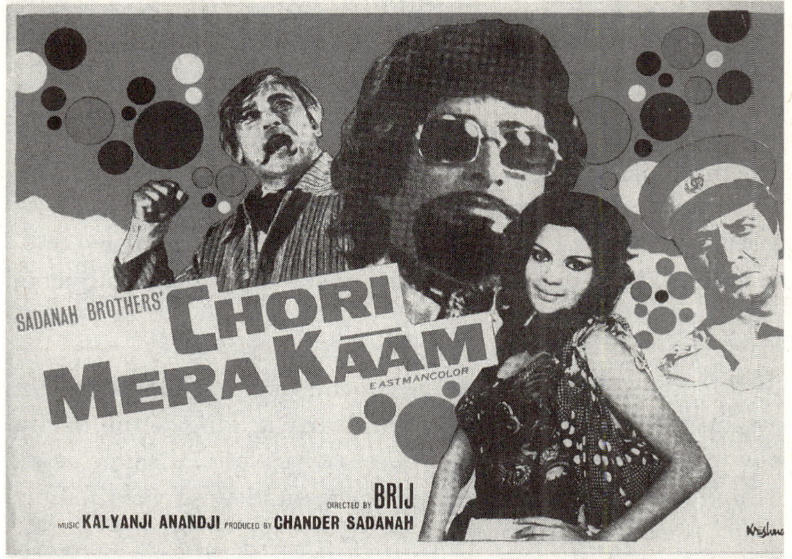

manuscript called *Chori Mera Kaam*. Bhola is the long-lost son of a police officer and has been raised by veteran thief Mr John (David Abraham). He commits petty robberies alongside his ex-girlfriend and partner-in-crime, Sharmili, while both of them also keep trying to con each other to amusing effect. During a heist, they discover an unpublished manuscript titled *Chori Mera Kaam*, a how-to guide on stealing. They sell it to a shady publisher, following which it becomes a nationwide bestseller for basically serving as an escape manual for criminals. The book's success and the spike in crime turn Bhola into a sudden celebrity. However, this newfound fame presents a myriad of challenges as Bhola quickly finds himself chased by various characters – police officers, gangsters and greedy opportunists – each with their own vendettas against him.

What ensues is a whirlwind of comedic mishaps, mistaken identities and unexpected reunions that keep the story engaging and fast-paced. True to the beloved tropes of classic Bollywood storytelling, the film weaves in a lost-and-found subplot that adds an emotional touch to the otherwise humorous chaos. During one hilarious and absurd scene in the romantic song '*Kahe Ko*' featuring the lead pair, Bhola offers Sharmili his heart, quite literally, with an actual beating heart shown on his outstretched palm.

By the time the film reaches its conclusion, all the loose threads are neatly resolved, resulting in heartwarming reunions and poetic justice. While the plot never strives for realism or depth, its main goal is to entertain, and it accomplishes this brilliantly.

A key reason for the film's lasting charm is its stellar ensemble cast, featuring some of Bollywood's most charismatic actors. Shashi Kapoor, known for his versatility, delivers an effortlessly charming portrayal as Bhola. He seamlessly balances mischief with vulnerability, making his character relatable and fun to watch. Despite playing the role of a petty thief, his engaging screen presence encourages the audience to rally behind him.

Although Zeenat Aman did not have a particularly substantial role, she adds a dose of glamour and chic to the film. Her chemistry with Shashi Kapoor creates a delightful dynamic, even if their romantic subplot isn't the main focus. Veteran actors Ashok Kumar and Pran bolster the film's narrative significantly. Pran, celebrated for his ability to add depth to any character, makes a memorable impact. Meanwhile, Ashok Kumar, with his commanding screen presence, skilfully blends crime and comedy, making his character both engaging and entertaining.

The supporting cast, featuring talents like Raza Murad, David, Deven Verma and Anwar Hussain, further boosts the film's energy. Each of them contributes their unique comedic touch to the movie, thereby ensuring that the humour remains lively and effective throughout. The collective synergy of the ensemble enriches the film's infectious charm, solidifying it as a complete entertainer.

No Bollywood masala film would be complete without a catchy soundtrack, and *Chori Mera Kaam* delivers on this front too. Composed by the legendary duo Kalyanji–Anandji, the film's music is vibrant and memorable, and it perfectly complements the film's playful spirit. The title track, also called '*Chori Mera Kaam*', quickly became a chart-topping hit upon its release and remains a cherished classic even today.

Brij Sadanah possessed an innate understanding of mainstream Bollywood cinema, and *Chori Mera Kaam* showcases his talent as a commercial film-maker. He wasn't one for experimenting with unconventional plots or artistic storytelling; instead, he often catered to the masses by delivering wholesome and engaging entertainment. With this movie, he skilfully balances multiple themes, including crime, humour and emotion, while also ensuring a titillating screenplay from start to finish. Despite the film's outlandish situations and unlikely coincidences, Brij's direction keeps the audience captivated. The humour predominantly stems from situational comedy rather than slapstick. Even the action sequences, while stylized in the quintessential Bollywood fashion of the 1970s, feel perfectly timed and never excessive.

His capacity to develop a screenplay that merges all the vital elements of a commercial hit – witty dialogues, amusing twists, gripping drama and chart-topping music – makes *Chori Mera Kaam* a quintessential example of his directorial skill.

Even fifty years after release, the film is fondly remembered by Bollywood enthusiasts. While today's moviegoers have become accustomed to crime comedies with more sophisticated storytelling and high production value, the film's humour and charm remain intact. It serves as a reminder of a time when Hindi cinema relied on straightforward narratives, exaggerated yet entertaining storytelling and pure star power to enthral audiences.

Tropes such as the lost-and-found narrative, over-the-top chase scenes and unexpected plot twists may appear outdated by modern standards, yet they remain appealing in their execution even today. The film is a nostalgic reminiscence of an era when Bollywood was all about grandiose storytelling that placed entertainment above rationality. The success it garnered at the box office was a testament to the timeless appeal of well-crafted comedy.

While *Chori Mera Kaam* can certainly not be considered a traditional classic, it truly embodies what makes classic Bollywood cinema so enchanting. Brij Sadanah's direction, the outstanding ensemble cast and Kalyanji-Anandji's spirited soundtrack come together to create a film that remains a beloved gem.

The allure of mid-1970s' Bollywood was its power to whisk audiences away to a world where anything could happen – where con artists could transform into bestselling authors, lost kids could find their families in the most unexpected ways and justice always arrives with a touch of humour. *Chori Mera Kaam* beautifully captures this essence, and it serves as a reminder of an era when viewers embraced fantasy wholeheartedly for the pure joy of cinematic magic. Perhaps that's the film's greatest appeal and the reason it continues to resonate.

CAST: Shashi Kapoor, Zeenat Aman, Pran, Ashok Kumar, Anwar Hussain, Raza Murad
OTHER CREDITS: Directed by Brij Sadanah. Music by Kalyanji Anandji.
RELEASE DATE: 2 May 1975
BOX OFFICE RESULT: Super Hit
RUNNING TIME: 2 Hours 37 Mins
TRIVIA: Brij Sadanah, the director known for films such as *Yeh Raat Phir Na Aayegi*, *Night in London*, *Do Ustad*, *Victoria No 203*, *Bombay 405 Miles* and *Ek Se Badhkar Ek*, had a violent end to his own life. On the night of Diwali in 1990 (21 October), in a drunken state, he shot his wife (actress Sayeeda Khan) and daughter to death before turning the gun on himself. His son, actor Kamal Sadanah, whose birthday it was the same day, survived with gunshot injuries to his neck.

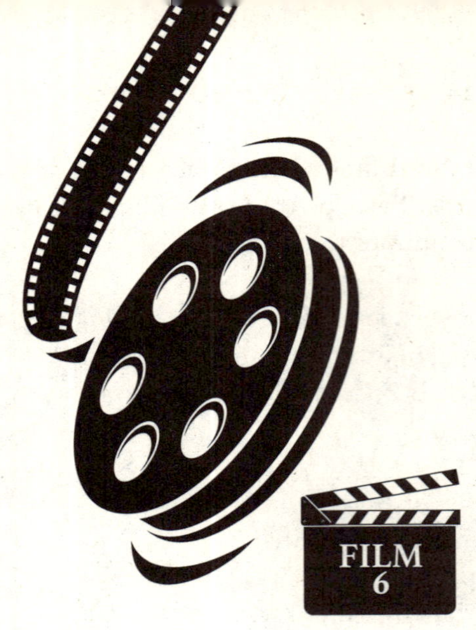

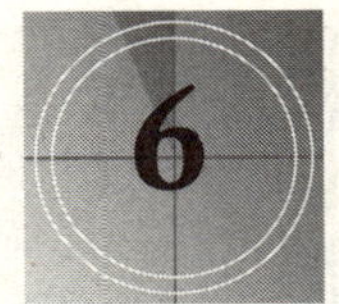

HRISHIKESH MUKHERJEE'S *CHUPKE CHUPKE*: A TIMELESS COMEDY

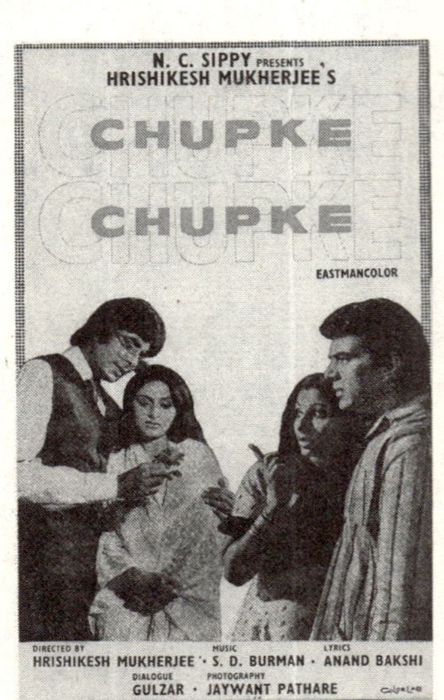

Released in 1975, Hrishikesh Mukherjee's *Chupke Chupke* is a charming comedy that has gracefully stood the test of time by continuing to enchant audiences. *Chupke Chupke* is based on the Bengali film *Chhadmabeshi*, featuring Uttam Kumar and Bikash Roy, with their Bollywood counterparts portrayed by Dharmendra and Om Prakash respectively. Known for his remarkable ability to blend humour with relatable storytelling, Mukherjee crafted a movie that

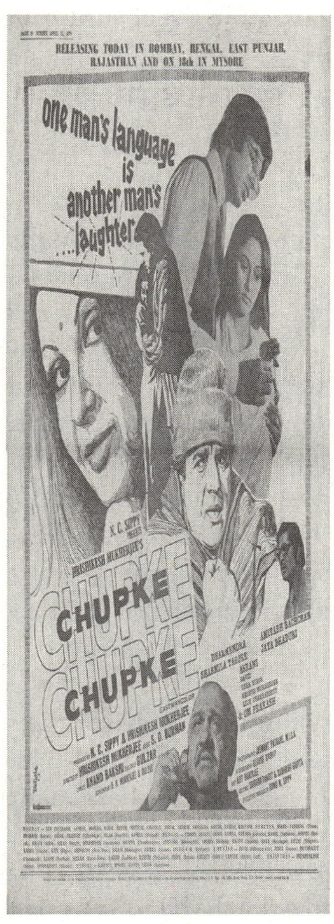

offers both endless laughs and deep insights into relationships and social quirks. Boasting an ensemble cast that included Dharmendra, Sharmila Tagore, Amitabh Bachchan, Jaya Bhaduri, Om Prakash and Asrani, this movie set a high benchmark for clever comedy in Indian cinema, with its amusing plotlines akin to those in Shakespearean comedies.

The narrative revolves around Professor Parimal Tripathi (Dharmendra), a botany teacher who marries Sulekha (Sharmila Tagore). To entertain himself while winning over his wife, Parimal devises a playful scheme against Sulekha's brother-in-law, Raghavendra Sharma (Om Prakash), who is a distinguished Hindi literature scholar greatly admired by Sulekha. Parimal disguises himself as a chauffeur named Pyare Mohan, enlisting the help of his friend Professor Sukumar Sinha (Amitabh Bachchan) to stand in for him. What follows is a delightful series of hilarious misunderstandings, clever dialogue and situational comedy as the characters become ensnared in a complicated web of trickery.

The comedy in *Chupke Chupke* is derived not from loud slapstick antics but from sharp wit, cultural subtleties and the absurdity of the situations that unfold. The light-hearted atmosphere mixed with the characters' endearing quirks makes the film an absolute joy to experience even today.

Hrishikesh Mukherjee, often dubbed the 'master of middle-of-the-road cinema', had an exceptional talent for narrating simple stories infused with emotional depth. Through *Chupke Chupke*, he displayed his prowess in depicting comical situations and expertly combined humour with a subtle social commentary. The film gently critiques the pretentiousness of academic elitism and the strictness of social traditions but does so with warmth rather than disdain. Mukherjee's direction is both subtle and powerful, which allowed the script and performers to shine. His careful attention to detail, showcasing everything from middle-class families to the complexities of human behaviour, infuses the film with authenticity. The pacing and comedic timing are impeccable, ensuring the film progresses smoothly without feeling forced.

The ensemble cast of *Chupke Chupke* showcases some of their most memorable performances. Dharmendra, typically known for his action-packed roles, captivates as the playful yet charismatic Parimal, whose comedic timing and chemistry with Sharmila Tagore's Sulekha are spot on. Amitabh Bachchan, in a supporting role, exhibits his versatility as the endearing yet hapless Sukumar. His exchanges with Jaya Bhaduri, who plays the woman he attempts to woo (but faces ridicule for being mistaken as the married Parimal), are filled with delightful banter and warmth.

Om Prakash, as the self-important Raghavendra, serves perfectly as a foil to the spirited younger cast. His confusion and frustration throughout the prank create an endless source of laughter.

Almost the entire film rests on the fabulous chemistry between him and Dharmendra. Asrani plays a smaller yet impactful role as a clumsy and comically awkward family friend, significantly enhancing the film's humour.

The music, composed by the legendary S.D. Burman, beautifully captures the film's light-hearted essence. Melodies like '*Ab Ke Sajan Saawan Mein*' and '*Chupke Chupke Chal Re Purvaiya*' are not only melodious but also complement the film's charm without disrupting the narrative flow.

Fifty years after it first appeared on screen, *Chupke Chupke* remains a cherished classic. Its comedy, rooted in simplicity and relatability, continues to resonate with audiences across generations. The film's emphasis on clean, family-friendly comedy sharply contrasts with the often brash and exaggerated humour prevalent in many contemporary films.

Chupke Chupke transcends being just a casual comedy; it celebrates human connections, the joy of innocent pranks and the importance of laughter in life. It embodies Hrishikesh Mukherjee's conviction in cinema's ability to entertain while subtly imparting essential life lessons and stands as a brilliant testament to the director's genius in creating timeless and sincere cinema. The film's ability to evoke smiles and warmth even after half a century. It is a film destined to be cherished for generations, proving that true comedy never fades.

CAST: Dharmendra, Sharmila Tagore, Amitabh Bachchan, Jaya Bhaduri, Om Prakash, Asrani, Keshto Mukherjee, David, Usha Kiron, Lily Chakraborty
OTHER CREDITS: Directed by Hrishikesh Mukherjee. Music by S.D. Burman.
RELEASE DATE: 11 April 1975
BOX OFFICE RESULT: Hit
RUNNING TIME: 2 Hours 26 Mins
TRIVIA: Amitabh Bachchan and Jaya Bhaduri almost forced Hrishikesh Mukherjee into taking them as the second leads. Hrishikesh felt the roles weren't meaty enough for them and wanted to cast newcomers, but both Amitabh and Jaya wanted to be a part of this film and didn't charge any remuneration.

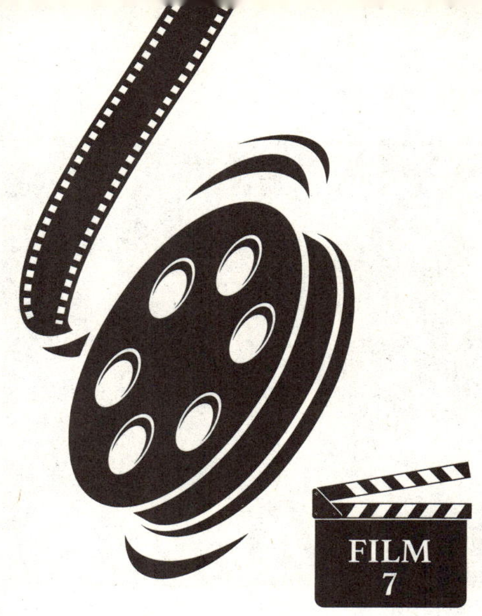

DEEWAAR: THE DEFINING MOMENT OF THE ANGRY YOUNG MAN IN HINDI CINEMA

Few films in the annals of Indian cinema have made as lasting an impact as *Deewaar*. Written by Salim–Javed and directed by the visionary Yash Chopra, this film is seen as the point in Bollywood's history when the 'angry young man' persona, first introduced in *Zanjeer* (1973), truly found both its voice and place in the heart of Bollywood. With its engaging story, morally complex characters and unforgettable dialogues that have etched themselves into India's cultural memory, *Deewaar* transcends mere cinema and serves as a mirror to the social and political turbulence of its time. This enabled it to strike a chord with the Indian middle class, providing a much-needed representation of their frustrations, worries and growing disillusionment.

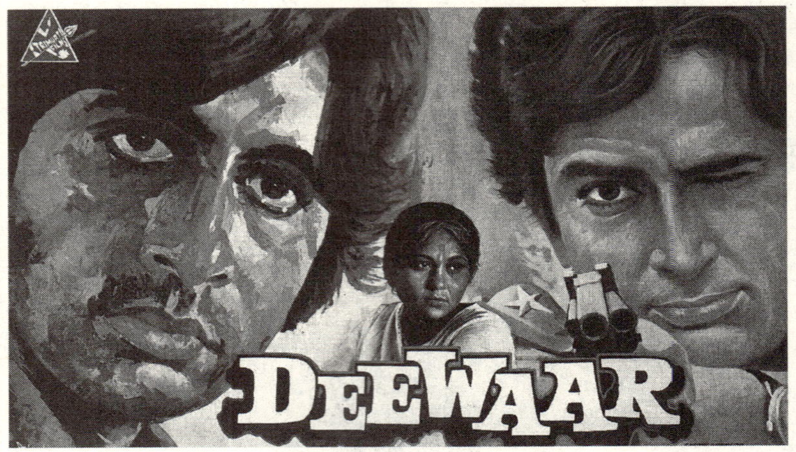

At its heart, *Deewaar* tells the tale of two brothers, Vijay (Amitabh Bachchan) and Ravi (Shashi Kapoor), whose lives take drastically different turns – one embraces the underworld, whereas the other dedicates himself to the pursuit of law and order. However, to frame the film as a simple battle of good versus evil would be oversimplifying its rich narrative. Unlike many conventional Bollywood films that typically present morality in stark contrasts, *Deewaar* explores the nuanced shades of grey. Vijay, although a criminal, evokes sympathy and connection, whereas Ravi, the law enforcer, grapples with challenging moral choices that put his beliefs to the test.

The film consistently probes the concept of morality through its diverse characters and situations. The boys' father, a labour-union leader, leaves his family vulnerable when faced with corporate threats, choosing personal safety over familial obligation. Vijay, marked by his father's cowardice and the hardships of his youth, turns to crime not for wealth but as a means to provide a better life for his mother and brother. Conversely, Ravi confronts ethical challenges of his own, especially when he crosses paths with the father of a young man he has fatally shot – a man who stole only to survive. The film does not offer simple solutions, but instead, it compels the audience to wrestle with these intricate moral dilemmas.

If *Zanjeer* marked Amitabh Bachchan's debut as the angry young man, *Deewaar* solidified his status as a superstar. Vijay Verma went on to become one of the most memorable characters in Indian cinema for deftly capturing the anger and helplessness of an entire generation. Born into hardship and burdened by his father's failures, Vijay carries the weight of his past like a visible scar. His journey from a struggling dockworker to a feared kingpin of crime is not only a tale of power but also a harrowing exploration of emotional anguish.

It is Vijay's complexity that draws viewers in. He is fierce when he needs to be, yet profoundly emotional concerning his mother (Nirupa Roy). One of the film's most unforgettable scenes that illustrates this duality is when he buys the very building where his mother once laboured. This is perceived as an act of defiance and victory as well as one steeped in love and yearning.

Amitabh Bachchan's commanding presence, paired with Salim-Javed's incisive dialogues, transformed Vijay into a cultural icon. Lines like '*Aaj mere paas building hai, property hai, bank balance hai, gaadi hai, bangla hai. Tumhare paas kya hai?*' (to which Ravi famously responds, '*Mere paas Maa hai*') have become a renowned part of cinematic lore, encapsulating the core emotional theme of the film in just a few words.

Shashi Kapoor's portrayal of Ravi serves as a perfect counterbalance

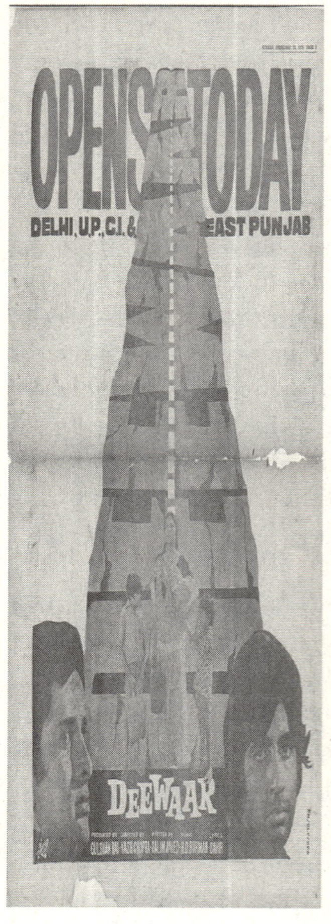

to Vijay. Where Vijay channels the frustration and rebellion of the working class, Ravi reflects the idealism and moral integrity of the law-abiding citizen. Yet he too faces his share of conflicts, as his choice to pursue his brother is not made easily. This represents the culmination of his moral quandaries, professional duty and the values instilled in him by their mother.

In one particularly moving scene, Ravi interacts with the father of a young thief who he has shot. The youth had only resorted to stealing to survive, and he paid the ultimate price for his desperation. Ravi's guilt and his realization that law and justice aren't always aligned add much depth to his otherwise virtuous character. His pursuit of Vijay comes not from hatred but from a painful necessity.

Nirupa Roy's role as the mother is crucial, both emotionally and thematically. She serves as the film's moral backbone, torn between her two sons – one who provides for her and the other who embodies her ideals. Her struggle revolves around impossible choices; for example, should she support the son who offers her comfort or align herself with the one who upholds the law? Her heartbreaking decision to distance herself from Vijay in his final moments is profound yet inevitable. This act symbolizes the film's central theme – morality extends beyond personal loyalty and involves advocating for something greater.

The 1970s in India were defined by social and political turmoil. Widespread economic disparity as well as rampant unemployment and corruption fuelled a growing sense of discontent among the middle and underprivileged classes. *Deewaar* tapped into this collective frustration, thereby making Vijay not just a character but a voice for the marginalized. His resistance to the establishment, rejection of conventional success and subsequent tragic downfall resonated deeply with the moviegoers of the time as they saw their own struggles reflected in his journey.

The film also explored the evolving moral landscape of urban India. Parveen Babi's character, Anita, showcases another facet of navigating the tough realities of Bombay (now Mumbai). Unlike the typical Hindi film heroine of that era, Anita is self-sufficient and daring, and her choices stem more from necessity than social norms.

While *Deewaar* is not a film led by music, it included two unforgettable songs – namely, '*Maine Tujhe Maanga*' and '*Kehdoon Tumhe*', composed by R.D. Burman and penned by Sahir. Although Salim–Javed initially intended for a song-free story, these songs, especially '*Kehdoon Tumhe*', offer brief moments of levity in the film's intensity.

Over the past fifty years, *Deewaar* has not only stayed relevant but has also woven itself into the very fabric of India's cinematic and cultural identity. The film's dialogues, themes and characters continue to inspire countless film-makers and audiences alike. This film transformed Bollywood in terms of storytelling, demonstrating that commercial cinema could be both smart and socially engaging.

More significantly, *Deewaar* provided the Indian audience with a hero they could connect with – one who was morally grey, who didn't always make the best decisions, but who reflected upon his struggles, frustrations and dreams. Extending beyond being merely a character, the angry young man became a cultural phenomenon, and *Deewaar* was the film that cemented the legacy of this character trope.

CAST: Shashi Kapoor, Amitabh Bachchan, Parveen Babi, Neetu Singh, Nirupa Roy, Madan Puri, Ifteqar, A.K. Hangal, Manmohan Krishna
OTHER CREDITS: Directed by Yash Chopra. Written by Salim-Javed. Music by R.D. Burman.
RELEASE DATE: 24 January 1975
BOX OFFICE RESULT: Blockbuster
RUNNING TIME: 2 Hours 54 Mins
TRIVIA: Rajesh Khanna was initially signed to play the role of Vijay and had been paid a signing amount as well. However, his failure to attend the script-reading sessions on three occasions led to the producer Gulshan Rai dropping him from the film, much to the delight of the writers Salim–Javed, who insisted on casting Amitabh Bachchan.

Waheeda Rehman and Vyjayanthimala were the original choices for the mother's role before Nirupa Roy was finalized.

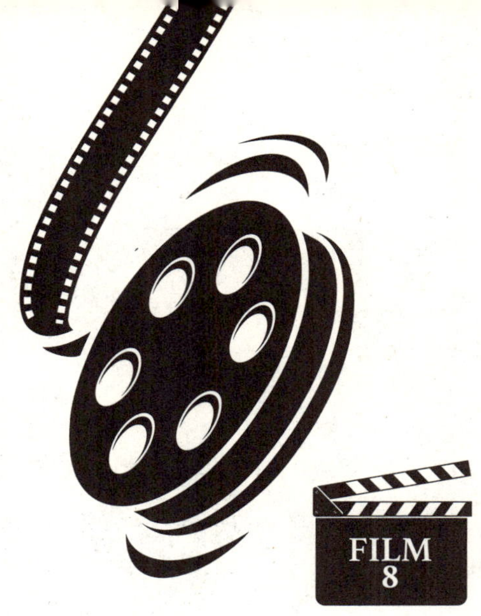

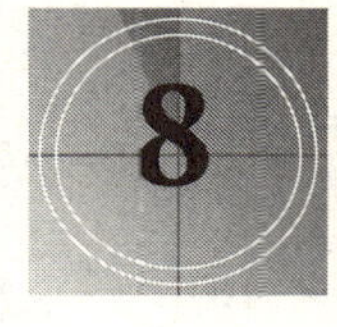

DHARAM KARAM: A MULTI-GENERATIONAL KAPOOR FAMILY PROJECT

Randhir Kapoor's *Dharam Karam* presents a captivating exploration of contrasts. As his second directorial venture following *Kal Aaj Aur Kal* (1971), in which he had the rare privilege of directing his illustrious father Raj Kapoor and his grandfather Prithviraj Kapoor at the young age of twenty-one, Randhir again took the helm to direct his father in *Dharam Karam*. This time, however, the storyline he chose bore a striking resemblance to one of Raj Kapoor's most influential films – *Awara* (1951) – yet diverged from it in significant ways. Both movies delve into the timeless debate surrounding nature versus nurture. While *Awara* champions nurture – implying that a person's surroundings dictate their fate – *Dharam Karam* flips the trope around. It contends that the essence of goodness or malice is ingrained in one's genes, independent of any environmental influences.

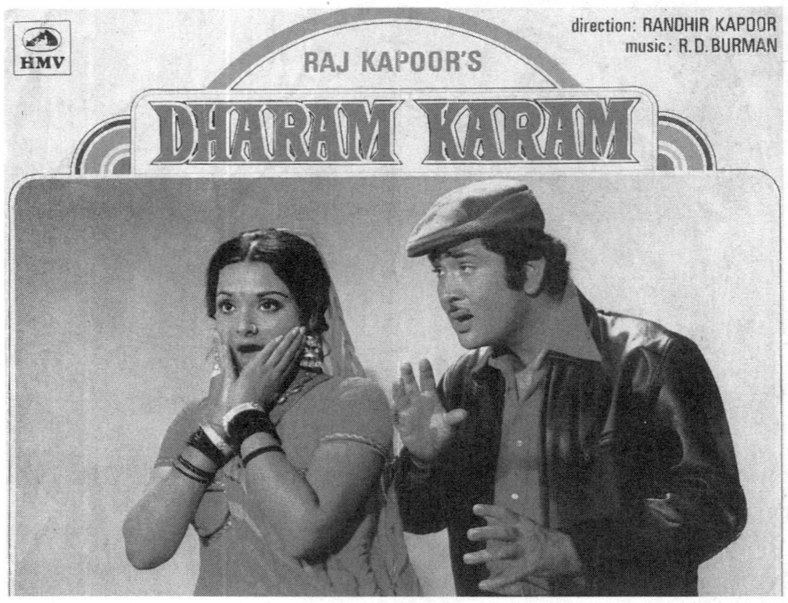

This thematic turn is important, as it not only challenges the philosophical foundations of *Awara* but also questions the broader Nehruvian socialist ideals that R.K. Films had come to represent. In *Dharam Karam*, the character Dharam (played by Randhir Kapoor) is swapped at birth by the criminal Shankar (Premnath) in a bid to taint the heritage of the upstanding Ashok (Raj Kapoor). Despite his upbringing in a world where he was expected to become a criminal, Dharam emerges as an inherently virtuous individual who is deeply passionate about music and has immense compassion for others. On the flip side, Ranjit (Narendranath), who is Shankar's biological son raised in Ashok's home, turns out to be a rogue. Through this contrast, the film raises an argument against the transformative capabilities of nurture, suggesting that inherent nature eventually seals one's destiny.

One of the most captivating features of *Dharam Karam* is how it deviates from the traditional ethos of R.K. Films. Unlike the emotionally driven and socially aware dramas typically associated with Raj Kapoor's productions, this film leans more towards the commercial formula of the 1970s – a blend of action, romance, music and comedy that dominated the Bollywood scene during that time. While R.K. Films had always managed to incorporate some level of mainstream appeal, *Dharam Karam* stands as a full-fledged masala entertainer that aligns more closely with the works of Manmohan Desai or Prakash Mehra than Raj Kapoor's introspective narratives.

The choices regarding casting and crew further emphasize this shift. Diverging from the practice of previous R.K. projects that favoured known in-house talent, *Dharam Karam* brought in new faces to the R.K. fold. The screenplay was crafted by Prayag Raaj, a writer more associated with mainstream commercial cinema than the poetic and (often) socialistic vision of Khwaja Ahmad Abbas, who had helped shape R.K.'s earlier films. R.D. Burman stepped in as the music director, replacing the long-standing duo of Shankar–Jaikishan, who had established the R.K. sound for many years. Even the leading lady, Rekha, marked a departure from the usual heroines of the Kapoor camp, such as Nargis or Vyjayanthimala (later Padmini Kolhapure). These changes highlighted an effort to bring R.K. Films into the modern age by aligning it with the evolving landscape of Bollywood instead of the socialist romanticism of Raj Kapoor's golden period.

One aspect of *Dharam Karam* that remains timeless is its music. The film's soundtrack by R.D. Burman features lyrics by Majrooh Sultanpuri and includes some beloved and memorable songs from the 1970s. The standout track '*Ek Din Bik Jayega Maati Ke Mol*' carries

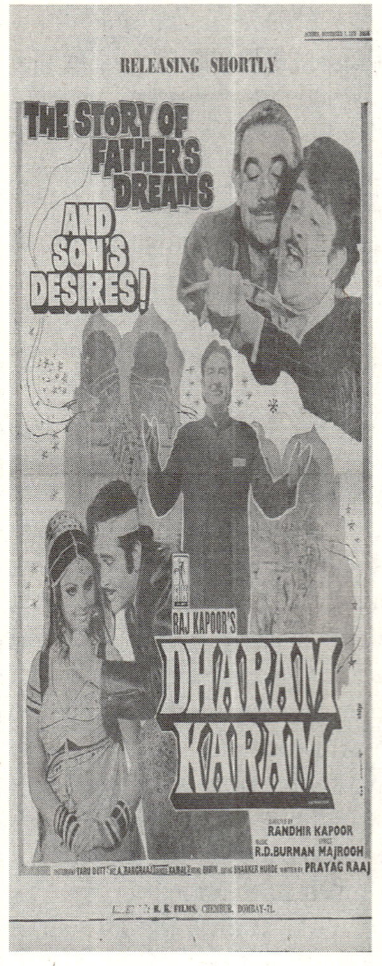

special significance as it was the last song Mukesh recorded for Raj Kapoor in a released film. Given the enduring emotional bond between Raj Kapoor and Mukesh, who was often regarded as the former's cinematic voice, this song invokes a deep sense of nostalgia. Moreover, it also serves as a farewell to an era that was drawing to a close.

Additional tracks, such as '*Tere Humsafar Geet Hai Tere*' and '*Baat Thi Ek Baer Ki*', are stereotypical examples of the spirit and vibrancy of 1970s' Bollywood. While the music of *Dharam Karam* may not have hit the same cultural heights as other films like *Bobby* (1973) or *Shree 420* (1955), it nonetheless stands as one of R.D. Burman's most noteworthy soundtracks.

When it was released in 1975, *Dharam Karam* enjoyed commercial success, although it never reached the iconic status of other R.K. Films classics such as *Awara*, *Shree 420*, or *Sangam*. Over time, however, it has successfully achieved a cult status primarily due to its unique position within the RK Films lineup. It is regarded as the most 'un-R.K.' film produced by the banner, which makes it very fascinating for Bollywood enthusiasts.

Looking back half a century later, *Dharam Karam* stands out not only for its themes but also for its reflection of the transitional phase of Bollywood. It debuted in the same year as *Deewaar*, which solidified Amitabh Bachchan's angry young man persona and marked a decline for Raj Kapoor's style of idealistic storytelling. In many respects, *Dharam Karam* feels like an experimental endeavour that attempts to modernize the R.K. brand while still retaining bits of emotional depth.

Nonetheless, Randhir Kapoor's twist on the 'nature versus nurture' debate in the film sparks further inquiry. While *Awara's* perspective on environmental influence seemed to fit in perfectly with the progressive socialist ideals of post-independence India, *Dharam Karam's* emphasis on the dominance of inherited nature speaks clearly of a more finalistic viewpoint. Does the film imply that individuals are *destined* to be either virtuous or villainous? And if it does, does that mean that the protagonists are thus absolved of any personal responsibility for their actions? These questions continue to render *Dharam Karam* an intriguing, albeit somewhat contentious, entry in Bollywood's lengthy history of moralistic storytelling.

Perhaps it is fitting that the film's most enduring song, *'Ek Din Bik Jayega Maati Ke Mol'*, serves as a reminder that all material success is fleeting. While *Dharam Karam* may not be the crown jewel of R.K. Films, it remains a compelling, if underrated, chapter in its storied history.

CAST: Raj Kapoor, Randhir Kapoor, Rekha, Premnath, Narendranath
OTHER CREDITS: Directed by Randhir Kapoor. Written by Prayag Raj. Music by R.D. Burman.
RELEASE DATE: 1 December 1975
BOX OFFICE RESULT: Average
RUNNING TIME: 2 Hours 41 Mins
TRIVIA: Narendranath, who was Premnath's younger brother in real life, played the role of his son in this movie. Both of them (along with their third brother, comedian Rajendranath) were the maternal uncles of Randhir Kapoor; their sister Krishna was married to Raj Kapoor.

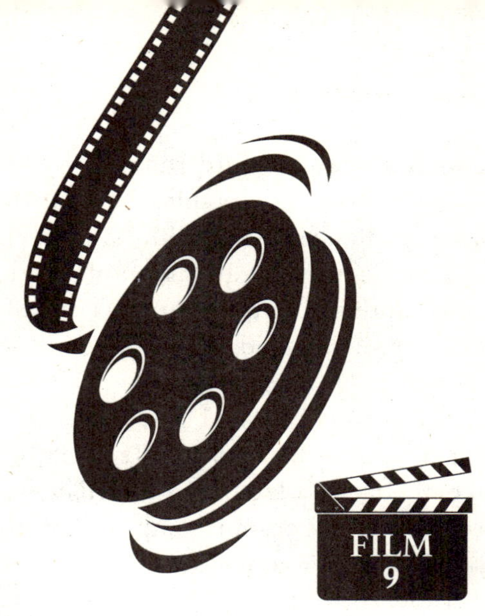

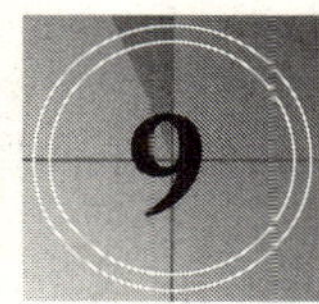

DHARMATMA: FEROZ KHAN'S STYLISH AND INDIANIZED ADAPTATION OF *THE GODFATHER*

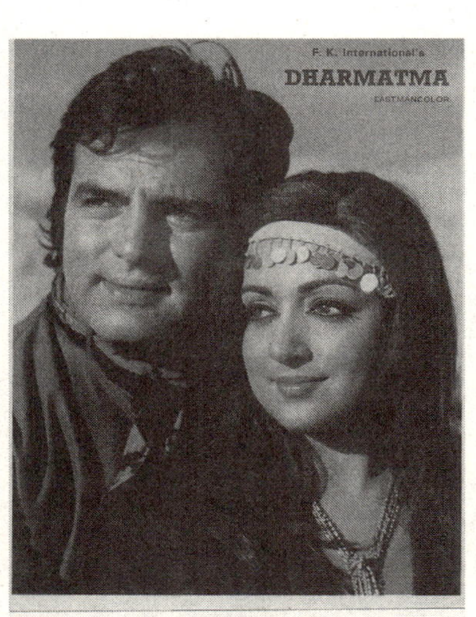

Feroz Khan's *Dharmatma* remains one of the most celebrated Bollywood films of its time that gained recognition for its gripping storyline, remarkable performances, stylish direction and memorable music. As India's first mainstream film to be shot extensively in Afghanistan, *Dharmatma* was inspired by Francis Ford Coppola's *The Godfather* (1972).

However, rather than being a straightforward remake, Khan restructured the film to fit within the Indian cultural context, making it deeply relatable to audiences here. With its perfect blend of action, drama and music, the film became a massive success at the box office and continues to be revered as one of the finest Indian adaptations of a Hollywood classic.

The film follows the story of Ranbir (played by Feroz Khan), the rebellious son of underworld kingpin Dharamdas (Premnath), known as Dharmatma. Like Michael Corleone in *The Godfather*, who initially hesitates to join his father's criminal empire, Ranbir is morally opposed to his father's illicit activities and distances himself from the world of crime. His inner conflict and strained relationship with Dharmatma drive the emotional core of the film.

Ranbir leaves his father's world and travels to Afghanistan, where he falls in love with a tribal girl named Reshma (Hema Malini). However, tragedy strikes when Reshma is killed, compelling Ranbir to return home and seek justice. As he reintegrates into the family, he discovers shocking betrayals and conspiracies, leading him to take over his father's empire in his own way. While the broad strokes of *Dharmatma* echo *The Godfather*, several key elements were altered to add Indian cinematic flavours – family values, melodrama and moral conflicts – ensuring a strong emotional connection with the audience.

Feroz Khan, who was not only the lead actor but also the director and producer, brought his own distinct style while creating *Dharmatma*. His direction was sleek and modern, introducing a level of visual flair rarely seen in Bollywood at the time. The film's outdoor sequences in Afghanistan, particularly in the stunning locales of Bamiyan and Kabul, added a fresh visual appeal that set it apart from the typical Bollywood gangster dramas of the era. Khan's direction demonstrates emotional depth, ensuring that apart from crime and power struggles, the story also includes themes of love, betrayal and redemption. His ability to blend action with emotion made the film more than just a crime saga; it also became a story about human relationships and moral dilemmas.

The film boasted a stellar ensemble cast, with each actor delivering power-packed performances. Premnath, as Dharmatma, played the authoritative yet emotionally vulnerable patriarch with great intensity. His performance gave the character a strong presence through a perfect balance between portraying menace and fatherly concern. Feroz Khan, as the reluctant heir Ranbir, portrayed a stylish yet intense character with aplomb, bringing a blend of charm and raw emotion to the role. Hema Malini's Reshma had a brief but impactful role as Ranbir's love interest and was pivotal to the film's plotline and emotional depth. Rekha played Anu, a woman who later enters Ranbir's life, which added another layer to his emotional journey. Lastly, Danny Denzongpa, Ranjeet, Dara Singh, Farida Jalal, Jeevan and Iftekhar contributed significantly to the film's success, playing characters that enriched the narrative with their unique portrayals of loyalty, betrayal and conflict.

One of the film's strongest elements was its music composed by the legendary duo Kalyanji–Anandji. The songs not only enhanced the narrative but also played an important part in the film's success. The songs *'Tumne Kisise Kabhi Pyar Kiya Hai'*, *'Tere Chehre Mein Wo Jadoo Hai'*, *'Mere Galiyon Se'* and *'Kya Khoob Lagti Ho'* are popular even today. Moreover, the background score significantly intensified the drama, especially during the action sequences and emotional confrontations.

Dharmatma was a huge box-office success, and it became a much-talked-about and beloved film. The film's stylish presentation, combined with its emotional weight, set a new benchmark for Bollywood crime dramas. The Indian audience connected deeply with its themes of family, morality and revenge, making it more than just an action-packed thriller.

What made *Dharmatma* stand the test of time was Feroz Khan's pioneering approach to film-making. His vision of an 'Indianized *Godfather*' was executed flawlessly while also ensuring that the film did not feel like a mere copy but rather a uniquely Indian story with universal appeal.

Five decades after its release, *Dharmatma* remains one of Bollywood's most elegant and well-crafted films. Feroz Khan's genius lay in his ability to adapt a Hollywood masterpiece while infusing it with Indian ethos, rich emotions and a gripping musical score. His directorial finesse, combined with powerful performances and an unforgettable soundtrack, cemented *Dharmatma* as a landmark film in Indian cinema. Even today, it is considered one of the best adaptations of *The Godfather*, proving that a great story, when adapted thoughtfully, can transcend cultural boundaries and stand the test of time.

CAST: Feroz Khan, Hema Malini, Rekha, Danny Denzongpa, Premnath, Ranjeet, Farida Jalal, Imtiaz Khan, Ifteqar, Dara Singh
OTHER CREDITS: Directed by Feroz Khan. Music by Kalyanji–Anandji.
RELEASE DATE: 30 April 1975
BOX OFFICE RESULT: Super Hit
RUNNING TIME: 2 Hours 39 Mins
TRIVIA: Ramesh Sippy's original choice to play the iconic role of Gabbar Singh in *Sholay* was Danny Denzongpa. However, Danny had to opt out of *Sholay* as he committed bulk dates to shoot in Afghanistan for *Dharmatma*.

Dharmatma was the first Hindi film that was shot extensively in Afghanistan.

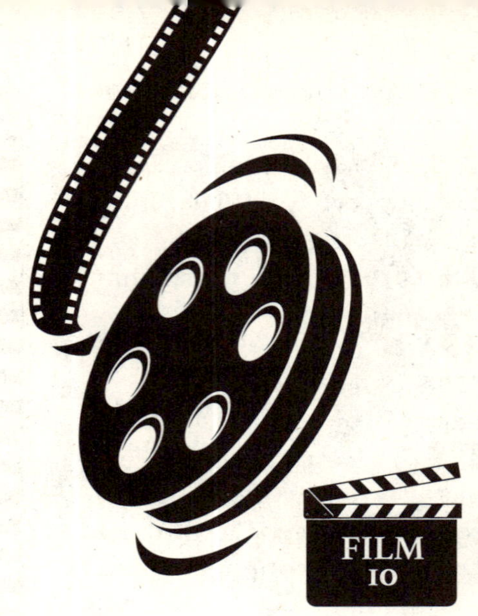

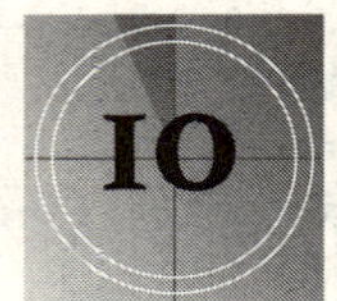

FARAAR: A TALE OF FATE, JUSTICE AND LOST LOVE

Shankar Mukherjee's *Faraar* is an engaging adventure film that mingles elements of crime thrillers with heartfelt domestic drama. Featuring notable performances by Amitabh Bachchan, Sharmila Tagore and Sanjeev Kumar, the film delves into profound themes such as justice, love, fate and ethical dilemmas. However, despite its captivating premise, *Faraar* struggles with a somewhat uneven execution, which made it difficult to solidify the film's position within either genre. Nevertheless, it remains an important milestone in Amitabh Bachchan's career and was also a key moment in his burgeoning stardom.

Faraar weaves a tale about the pitfalls of the justice system and the extreme lengths an average person will go to seek vengeance. The protagonist is Rajesh (Amitabh Bachchan) – an ordinary man

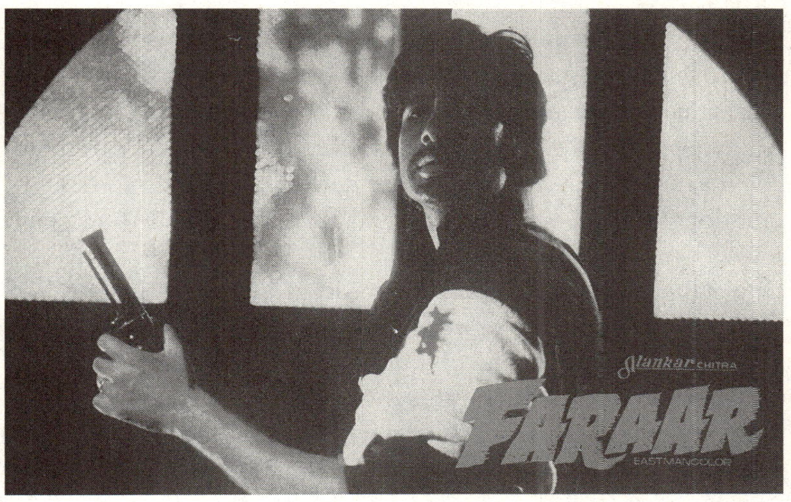

whose life is tragically thrown into chaos after his sister is brutally raped and murdered. The film highlights the shortcomings of the law enforcement system, which leave Rajesh frustrated and desperately seeking justice for his sister. This narrative is representative of the cinematic trends of the 1970s, a period when Bollywood increasingly began to portray protagonists in conflict with authority, as seen in films like *Deewaar*, *Zanjeer* and *Trishul*.

However, in contrast to the more assertive antiheroes featured in *Deewaar* or *Zanjeer*, Rajesh in *Faraar* is depicted as more passive. His pursuit of revenge stems from desperation rather than a defiance of the system. This shift distanced *Faraar* from the archetypal angry young man film and transformed it into a tragedy about a man who loses everything, including the love of his life, to a merciless twist of fate.

Another compelling aspect of *Faraar* is its ironic undertone. While on the run from the authorities, Rajesh unknowingly seeks shelter in the home of his former lover, Asha (now Mala), who is married to the very police officer who is hunting for him. This twist creates a tense atmosphere as Rajesh's presence threatens to unravel both his own existence and the peace of that household. The narrative hints at fate leading Rajesh towards a momentary emotional refuge, only to cruelly snatch it away by the film's end.

One of the main criticisms of *Faraar* is its inconsistency in tone. The film begins as a family drama, quickly morphing into a revenge-driven thriller before devolving into a tense, almost theatrical domestic drama. Although this multi-genre shift is an intriguing concept, it's not smoothly introduced in this film, resulting in a somewhat jarring transition. The dynamic between Rajesh and Sanjay – who remains oblivious to the fact that his guest is the fugitive he's pursuing – has its gripping moments, yet these are often overshadowed by the film's slower, melodramatic segments.

The domestic themes, albeit rich with emotion, lack the depth required to fully justify their prominence. Rajesh's connection with Mala and her young son is sincere but significantly disrupts the film's pacing. Furthermore, Sanjay's gradual realization of Rajesh and Mala's past is not sufficiently explored, making his eventual emotional turmoil seem abrupt. If the screenplay had offered a deeper exploration of these relationships, *Faraar* could have evolved into a more profound examination of fate and lost love rather than remaining an uneven thriller.

Despite its narrative shortcomings, *Faraar* is markedly elevated by the performances of its leading actors. Amitabh Bachchan, on the brink of superstardom with *Deewaar* and *Sholay*, both released that year, delivers a compelling performance. Contrasting with his fierier roles, Rajesh in *Faraar* is a man burdened by circumstance, and Bachchan successfully conveys his internal conflict through expressive body language instead of dramatic outbursts.

Sanjeev Kumar, celebrated for infusing depth into even the most poorly crafted roles, portrays Sanjay with a quiet intensity. His performance shines particularly in the film's latter half as he begins to unravel the truth about Rajesh. Rather than resorting to thunderous confrontations, Kumar's portrayal encapsulates a personal struggle that makes his character more relatable and grounded.

Sharmila Tagore, in the role of Mala, performs admirably, but her talent ultimately feels underutilized. Her character, caught between the past and present, holds significant potential, but the screenplay doesn't fully delve into her character's emotional depth. Unlike her more iconic roles in films like *Aradhana* or *Amar Prem*, her performance here, though sincere, doesn't leave a lasting impression.

The soundtrack of *Faraar*, composed by Kalyanji–Anandji, is largely forgettable, except for the memorable '*Main Pyaasa Tum Saawan*', which continues to resonate today. Beautifully sung by Kishore Kumar and Lata Mangeshkar, this song captures the nostalgia and longing inherent in Rajesh and Mala's relationship. Although *Faraar* didn't achieve the legendary status of Amitabh Bachchan's other 1975 films (*Deewaar*, *Sholay*, *Chupke Chupke*), it still holds an important position in his filmography. It marks a time when Bollywood began to experiment with genre-blending narratives, even if *Faraar* did so without success.

The film also draws comparisons to *Prem Kahani* (1975), another story that centred around love, sacrifice and tragic irony. In that film, the protagonist (also named Rajesh) unknowingly finds himself in the home of his ex-lover who is married to a police officer, only to face a tragic outcome. However, *Prem Kahani* focuses more on the emotional struggles and dilemmas of its three main characters, whereas *Faraar* finds its focus somewhat diluted.

Despite its flaws, *Faraar* is worth a watch, not only for Amitabh Bachchan's restrained performance but also for its ambitious – albeit ultimately unfulfilled – attempt to merge thriller elements with emotional drama. It serves as a reminder of a period in Bollywood when film-makers dared to take creative risks, even if those endeavours didn't always culminate in a fully cohesive cinematic experience.

CAST: Sanjeev Kumar, Amitabh Bachchan, Sharmila Tagore, Rajan Haskar, Murad
OTHER CREDITS: Directed by Shankar Mukherjee. Music by Kalyanji–Anandji.
RELEASE DATE: 21 November 1975
BOX OFFICE RESULT: Below Average
RUNNING TIME: 2 Hours 36 Mins
TRIVIA: The film was very loosely based on the 1964 Hollywood thriller *Signpost to Murder*, which was adapted more directly by Yash Chopra for his 1969 thriller *Ittefaq*.

Amitabh Bachchan and Sharmila Tagore had another release in the same year, *Chupke Chupke*, although they were not paired opposite each other in that. They later did one more film, *Besharam*, in 1978.

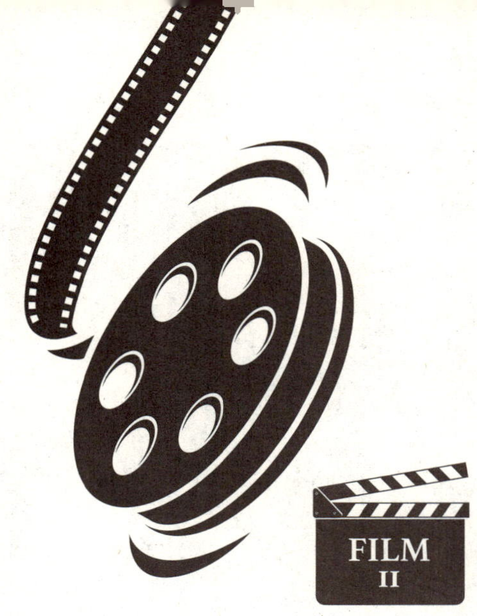

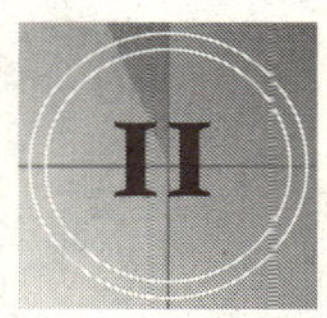

GEET GAATA CHAL: HIREN NAG'S BREEZY SONG OF LIFE

Rajshri Productions has always been a name that makes films celebrating the warmth of human connections, the beauty in life's simple pleasures and the charming aspects of everyday existence. During an era when mainstream Hindi cinema was largely focused on action-driven plots and intense dramas like *Sholay* and *Deewaar*, *Geet Gaata Chal* emerged as a breath of fresh air. Directed by Hiren Nag, this film encapsulated everything that Rajshri stood for – innocence, love, family ties and a sincere connection with rural India. Released in a time when action films dominated the box office, this modestly produced, emotionally rich film became significantly successful, demonstrating that at its essence and irrespective of its genre, cinema thrives on storytelling that truly strikes a chord with viewers.

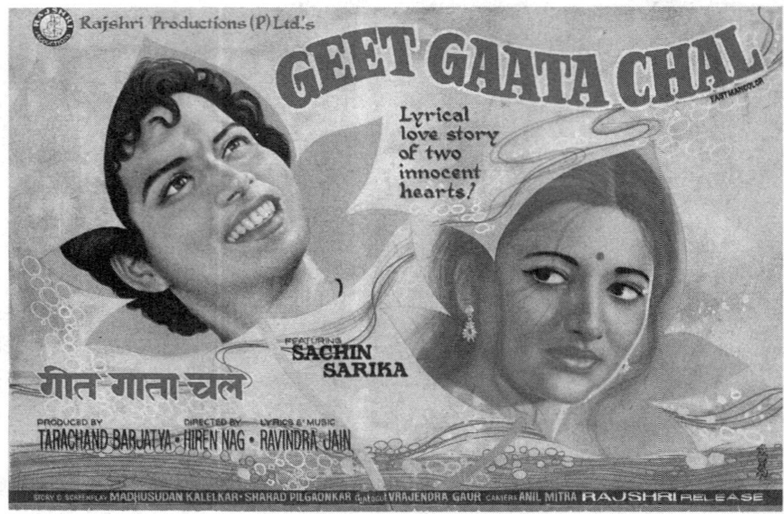

At the heart of this enchanting narrative is Shyam, portrayed by Sachin, a free-spirited young man who feels most at home on the open roads. A wandering minstrel, he carries no burdens, no attachments and no worries – just his music and an infectious love for life. He travels from village to village, spreading joy through his songs wherever he wanders. Adapted from Rabindranath Tagore's short story 'Atithi', the film gently explores this nomadic spirit, making Shyam appear more than just a character; he becomes a symbol of unfettered freedom and a life unbothered by the weight of expectations and responsibilities. His carefree nature and golden-hearted spirit win the affection of all, and it is this quality that draws him into the embrace of a warm, loving family. They welcome him with open arms, showering him with kindness, and for a brief moment, it seems he might finally discover a sense of belonging.

However, life is not so straightforward, and emotions are rarely predictable. Radha, played by Sarika in one of her early adult performances, initially feels resentment towards Shyam's presence in her home. The love and attention he receives from her parents trigger feelings of jealousy, thus prompting her to make his life difficult in any way she can. However, hostility often hides seeds of unexpected affection; as time weaves their lives together, Radha's resentment gradually transforms into a love so intense that she finds herself irresistibly drawn to him. Her parents, observing the blossoming bond, are thrilled at the thought of their daughter marrying this kind and genuine young man. Although everything appears perfect, this newfound love, along with the possibility of a settled life, becomes an overwhelming source of fear for Shyam.

For someone who has only tasted the joys of wandering freely, the idea of being anchored down is unimaginable. The mere thoughts of permanence and of being tied to expectations and responsibilities sends him into a panic. Hence, he instinctively does what he knows best – he runs. Just as he always moved from one place to another in the past, he drifts away once more, leaving behind a heartbroken Radha, a family who cherished him and a love story that now seems fated to remain unfinished. The emotional heartbeat of the film lies in the questions it raises: Does Radha's love bring Shyam back, or does he remain true to his restless heart? Can love tame the wind, or does the wind forever resist being captured?

Geet Gaata Chal is much more than a love story. The film offers a thought-provoking reflection on the essence of freedom and

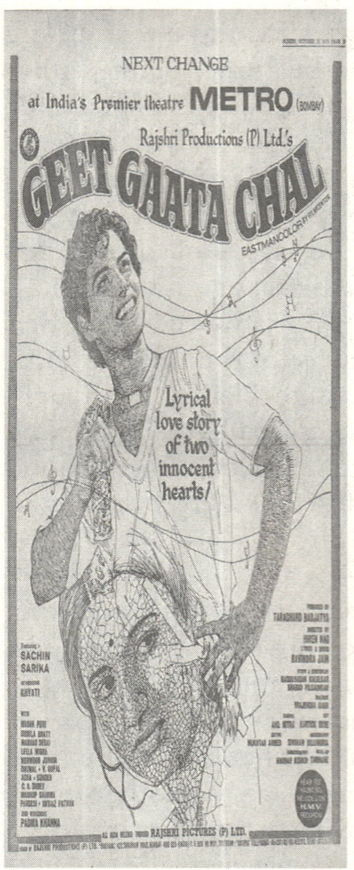

bonding. Through Shyam's character, the film poses a vital question – does true happiness lie in the comfort of home and relationships or in the liberated embrace of the broader world? For Radha, love is synonymous with togetherness, whereas for Shyam, love cannot equate to a loss of freedom. This intricate conflict, beautifully woven throughout the narrative, enhances the film's enduring charm. Even today, it connects with anyone who has grappled with the desire to feel connected while fearing the constraints of commitment.

Intensifying the film's timeless appeal is its stunningly simple yet visually vibrant portrayal of rural India. Rajshri Productions has always excelled in presenting idyllic village scenes, and *Geet Gaata Chal* is no exception. The lush green fields, twisting paths and tranquil rivers – every scene is infused with a peace that enables the audience to feel as if they are part of this beautiful, pristine world. The cinematography captures the spirit of the countryside, depicting it as not only a background but also a vital element of the film's essence.

The grounded simplicity of village life, the innocence of its inhabitants and their deep-rooted traditions are brought to life with an authenticity that makes the film feel like a soothing lullaby – gentle, comforting and nostalgic.

Perhaps the most unforgettable element of *Geet Gaata Chal* is its music. Ravindra Jain's compositions are enchanting and vital in shaping the film's emotional mood. The title track, '*Geet Gaata Chal*', perfectly embodies Shyam's wandering spirit and establishes the tone for the entire film. The track '*Shyam Teri Bansi*' stands out for capturing the beauty of love and longing in a haunting melody. And then there's '*Ram Sia Ram*', a *bhajan* that has become a widely known and cherished devotional song among listeners. Jaspal Singh shot to fame with his melodious renditions of the superhit songs of this film.

The performances contribute significantly to the film's charm. Sachin, with his youthful innocence and natural acting, makes Shyam utterly endearing. His depiction of a free-spirited wanderer is so genuine that it's hard to picture anyone else in the role. Sarika too delivers a performance imbued with raw emotion and a disarming innocence, seamlessly transitioning from jealousy to love to heartbreak. Together they bring to life a love story that is as sweet as it is poignant. The supporting cast also appears warm and authentic, further amplifying the narrative and making every relationship in the film feel lifelike and relatable.

The success of *Geet Gaata Chal* serves as a testament to the impact of simple storytelling. It proved that a film need not be packed with high-octane drama or grand heroes to win over hearts. At its essence, cinema revolves around emotions – which makes films connect deeply with audiences – and that is precisely what *Geet Gaata Chal* accomplished.

In an era when commercial cinema was shifting towards darker, more action-packed stories, this film beautifully highlighted the enduring charm of love, music and genuine human connections. It illustrated that even amid the chaos, there is always room for quiet, soulful narratives that serve as reminders of all the good that still exists in the world.

Geet Gaata Chal remains a widely admired classic. Its melodious soundtrack can still be heard in homes today; its themes continue to resonate deeply, and its characters have carved a special place in the hearts of those who first experienced its enchantment. This film speaks to the soul by radiating the pure joy that comes from navigating life through song, carefree and liberated. It is a film that, much like Shyam himself, refuses to fade away, forever wandering in the hearts of those who experience it even once.

CAST: Sachin, Sarika, Urmila Bhatt, Leela Mishra, Madan Puri, Padma Khanna
OTHER CREDITS: Directed by Hiren Nag. Music by Ravindra Jain.
RELEASE DATE: 16 October 1975
BOX OFFICE RESULT: Super Hit
RUNNING TIME: 2 Hours 11 Mins
TRIVIA: The late Australian rapper Hunter's song 'Puncheon' was inspired by the title song of *Geet Gaata Chal*.

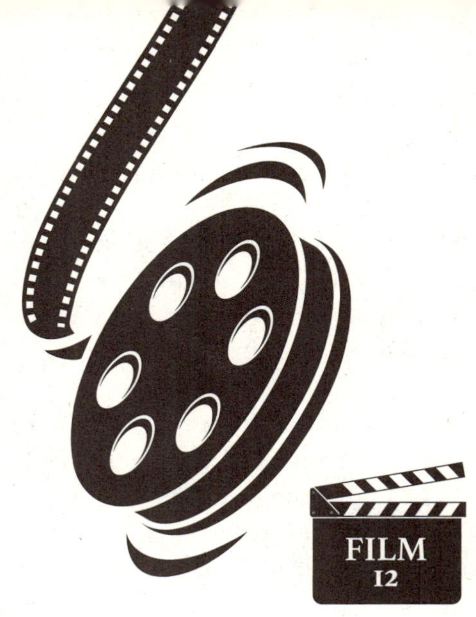

JAI SANTOSHI MAA: THE MYTHOLOGICAL MASTERPIECE THAT CHALLENGED *SHOLAY*

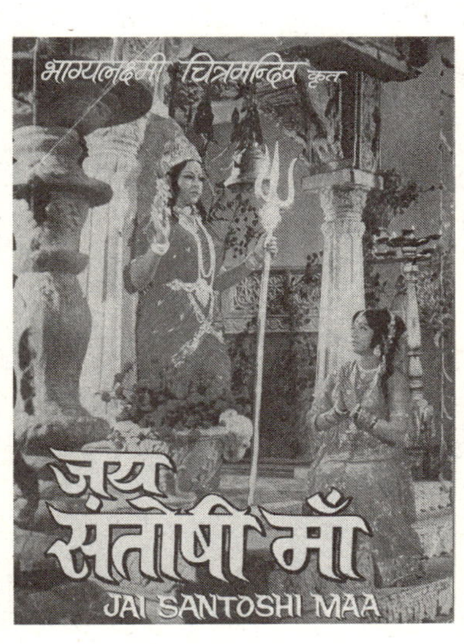

Indian cinema has witnessed many unexpected success stories, but few can match the sheer astonishment that accompanied the rise of *Jai Santoshi Maa*. Released alongside the towering blockbuster *Sholay*, a film that redefined the action genre and was backed by industry stalwarts, *Jai Santoshi Maa* was an unlikely competitor. This low-budget mythological film with no major stars was directed by then unknown Vijay Sharma and produced by Satram Rohra. The film had no initial promise of commercial success; however, through its depiction of the power of faith and devotion as well as word-of-mouth recommendations by initial audiences, it not only held its ground but surprisingly turned out to be a cultural and social phenomenon.

At a time when spectacle-driven films dominated the box office, *Jai Santoshi Maa* appeared in stark contrast. It had none of the grand sets, action sequences, or high-voltage drama that defined Bollywood's commercial ventures. Instead, it relied on simple storytelling, a strong devotional fervour and the highly moving power of faith.

The film was based on the folk mythology of Santoshi Maa, a relatively lesser-known Hindu goddess whose worship had not yet gained widespread recognition in India before the movie. Unlike mainstream mythological deities in Hinduism like Durga, Kali or Lakshmi, Santoshi Maa's legend was propagated orally through household narratives, particularly among women from lower-and middle-class backgrounds. The film presented the goddess as a symbol of patience, perseverance and divine justice – virtues that aligned perfectly with the beliefs of its target audience.

Despite its spiritual appeal, the film initially had a slow and underwhelming start. Its first three days saw dismal collections that barely reached the hundreds. Given that 1975 was a year of cinematic landmarks, with *Sholay* and *Deewaar* dominating the scene, *Jai Santoshi Maa* seemed like it was destined for obscurity. However, something extraordinary happened among audiences, particularly women, who started flocking to the film in droves.

The transformation from an ignored release to a cultural sensation was nothing short of miraculous. Word-of-mouth spread like wildfire, and soon, cinema halls screening *Jai Santoshi Maa* became packed. A significant portion of the audience consisted of devout women who saw the film not just as entertainment but as an act of religious devotion. Theatres across India witnessed an unusual phenomenon in which audiences began removing their footwear before entering the cinema hall, a gesture that is traditionally reserved for places of worship.

This fervour turned *Jai Santoshi Maa* into a cult classic. No longer just a film, it began being perceived as a religious experience. Many viewers claimed to have undergone spiritual awakenings while watching it, reinforcing the film's reputation as a divine spectacle. The film's impact extended beyond the screen as newly turned devotees of the goddess began initiating Santoshi Maa pujas in their homes, temples started being built in her name and women began observing fasts dedicated to the goddess. In many ways, *Jai Santoshi Maa* did not just reflect devotion but also created it.

A significant element of *Jai Santoshi Maa* was its music composed by C. Arjun with lyrics by the legendary Kavi Pradeep. The songs, performed by Usha Mangeshkar, Manna Dey and Mahendra Kapoor, became anthems of ardent devotion. The most iconic among them, '*Main Toh Aarti Utaaroon Re Santoshi Mata Ki*', transcended the cinematic medium and entered the realm of religious hymns. To date, the song continues to be played in temples, household prayer ceremonies and religious gatherings, making it one of the most popular bhajans among Hindu Indians.

Kavi Pradeep's lyrics captured the essence of unwavering faith, while C. Arjun's compositions ensured that the music was deeply immersive and invoking a sense of devotion among listeners. Thus, the soundtrack became one of the major reasons for the film's longevity.

The most fascinating aspect of *Jai Santoshi Maa's* success was its influence on India's Hindu population. Films often draw from cultural beliefs, but rarely do they create religious movements. This film, however, was critical in popularizing the worship of Santoshi Maa, a goddess who, until then, had remained largely confined to oral traditions and localized faith practices.

The film also highlighted the role of women as the primary carriers of devotion in Indian society. It was largely female audiences who contributed to the film's massive success, introducing the unprecedented idea that cinema could also be a medium of spiritual engagement.

It is impossible to discuss this film without acknowledging its release alongside *Sholay*, one of the biggest and most famous blockbusters in Indian film history. While *Sholay* was an extravagant production featuring a stellar cast, grand action sequences and a gripping narrative, *Jai Santoshi Maa* was a humble devotional film that relied purely on faith-driven storytelling. Nonetheless, the fact that it held its own against the megahit *Sholay* at the box office demonstrated its extraordinary pull.

Sholay catered to audiences seeking action and drama, whereas *Jai Santoshi Maa* appealed to the spiritual and devotional instincts of the masses. In doing so, it carved a niche in Indian cinema that no other film of its kind had achieved before. Despite its modest budget and lack of big names, this movie surprisingly emerged as one of the highest-grossing films of the year.

The legacy of *Jai Santoshi Maa* endures even today and remains a benchmark for mythological cinema, setting a novel demand for devotional films in Bollywood. Its success paved the way for numerous religious films in the subsequent decades, although few could replicate its widespread impact.

Even in the modern era, wherein mythological films are often relegated to TV or digital platforms, the story of *Jai Santoshi Maa* highlights the previously unknown and unbreakable bond between faith and cinema. It showed the Hindi movie industry that sometimes, the most unexpected films can leave the deepest impact, and devotional cinema can tap into something far more profound than the human soul.

CAST: Anita Guha, Ashish Kumar, Bharat Bhushan, Kanan Kaushal, Rajan Haskar
OTHER CREDITS: Directed by Vijay Sharma. Music by C. Arjun.
RELEASE DATE: 30 May 1975
BOX OFFICE RESULT: Blockbuster
RUNNING TIME: 2 Hours 25 Mins
TRIVIA: Anita Guha, who played the role of Santoshi Maa in the film, was the maternal aunt of actor Prema Narayan.

After watching the movie, it is reported that people would come to Anita Guha's house to seek her blessings.

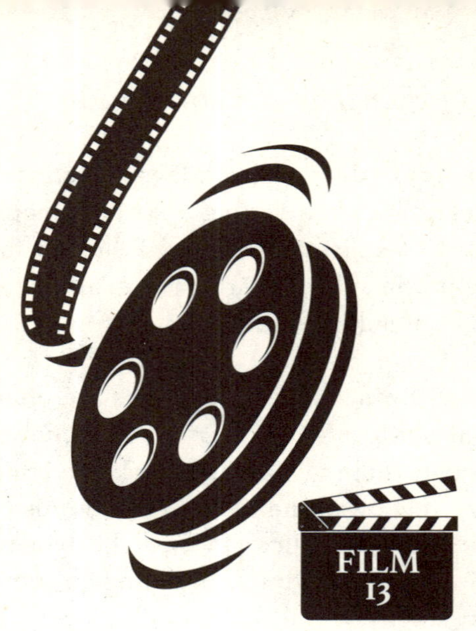

B. NAGI REDDY'S *JULIE*: A PIONEERING EXPLORATION OF LOVE, IDENTITY AND SOCIAL NORMS

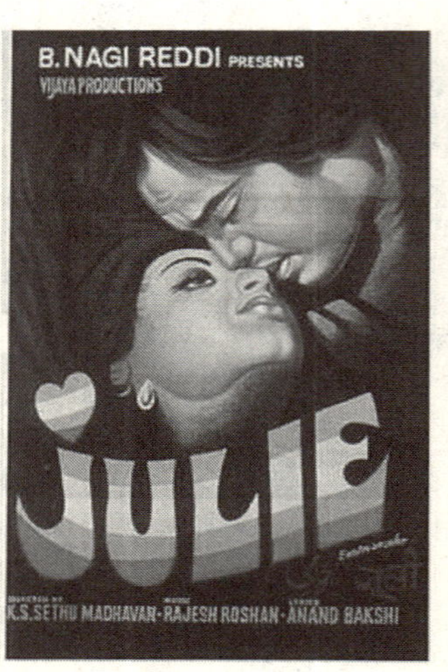

B. Nagi Reddy's *Julie*, directed by K.S. Sethumadhavan, was a ground-breaking film in Hindi cinema for being way ahead of its time. Remade from the Malayalam original *Chattakkari* (1974), the film boldly addressed themes of pre-marital pregnancy, interfaith relationships and societal double standards at a time when mainstream Hindi cinema often shied away from such topics. With a stellar cast including Lakshmi, Vikram, Nadira,

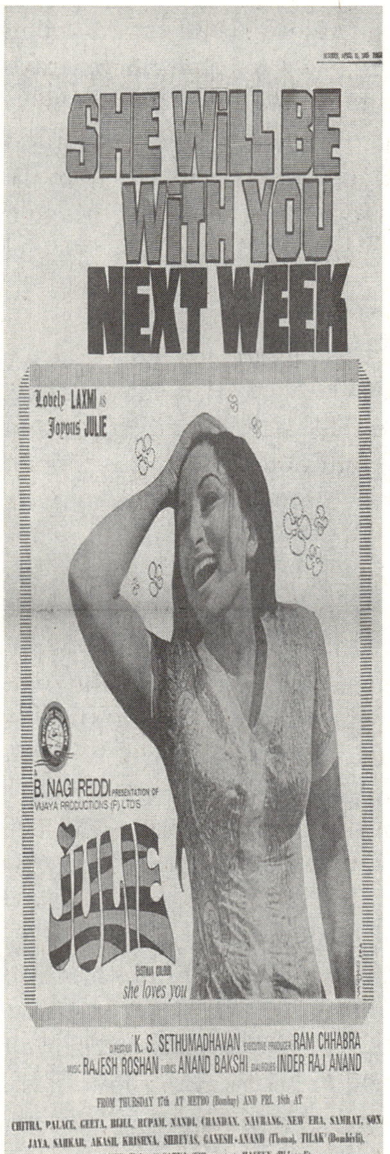

Om Prakash, Utpal Dutt and Rita Bhaduri, *Julie* remains a landmark film that seamlessly integrated socially relevant themes within a commercial context, achieving both critical praise and widespread appeal.

At its heart, *Julie* is a touching examination of love that transcends religious and social divides. Julie, a young Christian woman, falls for Shashi, a Bengali Hindu Brahmin man, resulting in an unexpected pregnancy that disrupts her life dramatically. The film explores the intricacies and challenges of social norms, the stigma surrounding pre-marital pregnancy and the strict moral codes enforced upon women. Set in the conservative landscape of the 1970s, where female virtue and family honour were of utmost importance, *Julie* was ingenious in portraying a woman's journey as she faced these challenges.

The film also provides a

nuanced depiction of religious and cultural conflicts. Although interfaith romances were not entirely new to Hindi cinema (with films like *Dhool Ka Phool* (1959) and *Garm Hava* (1973) touching upon similar themes), *Julie* distinctively represented the cultural values of the Anglo-Indian and Christian communities in India. While it did rely on some familiar tropes – such as a focus on Westernized lifestyles and a moralistic undertone – its portrayal remained rich and genuine for its era.

Lakshmi, reprising her role from *Chattakkari*, delivered a heart-wrenching performance as Julie. Her portrayal of vulnerability, resilience and innocence made the character both relatable and sympathetic. Vikram, as Shashi, contributed effectively, though his character was more reactive than proactive throughout the story.

Nadira's stunning performance as Julie's demanding mother successfully captured the essence of a mother caught between conforming to social expectations and love for her child. Om Prakash and Utpal Dutt, as parental figures, brought a mix of humour and depth that enhanced the film's narrative. Rita Bhaduri, who plays Julie's encouraging friend, added the much-needed warmth to the storyline and offered a contrast to the older generation with their stringent moral expectations.

One of the standout features of *Julie* its music composed by then-unknown Rajesh Roshan, marking his debut as a music director. The soundtrack was a tremendous hit, with songs that have resonated across generations. Tracks like '*Yeh Raatein Nayi Purani*', '*Bhool Gaya Sab Kuch*', '*Dil Kya Kare*' and the English number 'My Heart Is Beating' remain popular among listeners. Rajesh Roshan's music played a vital role in shaping the film's emotional atmosphere, which made *Julie* as much a musical triumph as it was a cinematic one.

While *Julie* offers a somewhat stereotypical depiction of the Christian community, it opened the door for more nuanced representations in later films. Basu Chatterjee's *Baaton Baaton Mein* (1979) provided a more genuine and everyday portrayal of an Anglo-Indian family that is free from the melodramatic conflicts seen in *Julie*. Nonetheless, *Julie* deserves recognition for bringing a marginalized community into mainstream Hindi cinema.

In terms of its social commentary, *Julie* was ahead of its time. Subsequent films like *Kya Kehna* (2000) and *Salaam Namaste* (2005) revisited the topic of unplanned pregnancy, but *Julie* did so in an era when such discussions were almost taboo. Although the film didn't entirely evade moral scrutiny – such as how Julie's mother's ultimate acceptance of her daughter is still portrayed within the framework of social reconciliation rather than pure female empowerment – it successfully sparked an important conversation.

Five decades later, *Julie* still holds relevance. Its themes of love versus societal norms, gender expectations and the stigma surrounding unwed mothers remain pertinent in today's discourse. While its dramatic execution may seem somewhat dated, the film's emotional essence and its willingness to confront challenging topics make it a significant milestone in Indian cinema.

Ultimately, *Julie* endures not only for its trailblazing subject matter but also for its engaging storytelling, unforgettable performances and timeless music, which is a testament to its lasting influence.

CAST: Lakshmi, Vikram, Om Prakash, Nadira, Utpal Dutt, Rita Bhaduri, Sridevi
OTHER CREDITS: Music by Rajesh Roshan.
RELEASE DATE: 18 March 1975
BOX OFFICE RESULT: Super Hit
RUNNING TIME: 2 Hours 25 Mins
TRIVIA: The movie's English song 'My Heart Is Beating' is possibly the first full English song in a Hindi movie. The song was written by Harindernath Chattopadhyay and was sung by Preeti Sagar.

A young Sridevi, aged eleven or twelve at the time, plays the role of Irene, who is Julie's younger sister. This was Sridevi's first significant role in a Hindi film as a child artist. Her character, Irene, is part of Julie's Anglo-Indian family and appears in several family scenes in a supporting role.

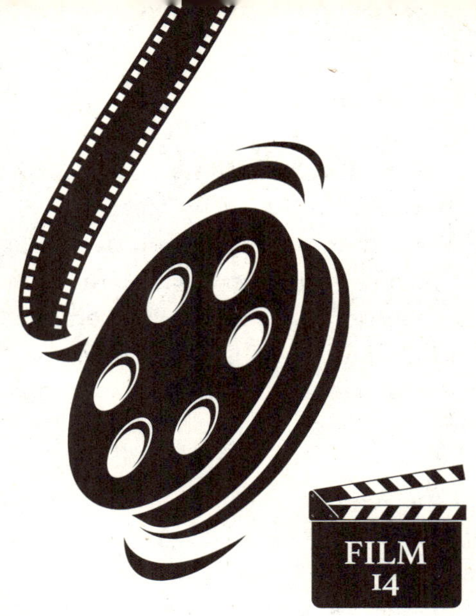

RAVIKANT NAGAICH'S *KAALA SONA*: OF DESI COWBOYS, GLAMOUR DOLLS AND A VILLAIN NAMED POPPY SINGH

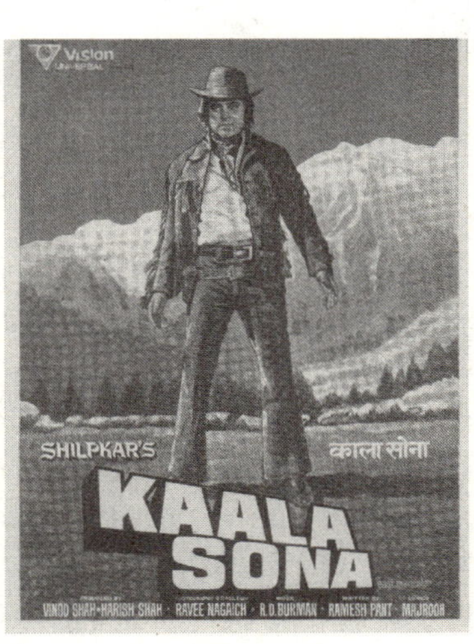

Ravikant Nagaich's *Kaala Sona* stands out as a unique film in the Indian commercial cinema of the time. The film successfully blends the gritty, sun-drenched aesthetic of spaghetti westerns with the vibrant, high-energy entertainment of Bollywood, thereby solidifying its place as a cherished cult classic in Bollywood history. With its striking visuals, larger-than-life performances and an unforgettable soundtrack, the film captures the adventurous essence of mid-1970s' Bollywood. Produced by Harish Shah, directed by cinematographer Ravikant Nagaich and featuring music by the legendary R.D. Burman, *Kaala Sona* is brought to life by a dynamic cast. The cast featured Feroz Khan, Parveen Babi, Danny Denzongpa, Farida Jalal and Prem Chopra, who come together in a spirited revenge drama set against an unconventional backdrop of the opium trade and human trafficking.

By the time *Kaala Sona* hit the screens, Feroz Khan had firmly established himself as Bollywood's version of the Western anti-hero. His good looks, charisma, effortless flair and affinity for stylish action roles made him carve a niche for himself in Hindi cinema. Together with *Khote Sikkay* (1974) and later *Kachche Heere* (1981), *Kaala Sona* forms an unofficial trilogy that could be labelled as Khan's most notable 'curry western' films. The influence of Clint Eastwood's iconic *Man with No Name* from Sergio Leone's spaghetti westerns can be felt in Khan's portrayal. He embodies a rugged yet introspective hero, a lone figure who is a man of few words but acts swiftly and decisively. However, unlike the grim themes prevalent in Leone's films, *Kaala Sona* retains the true spirit of Bollywood, with Khan's character, despite his tough demeanour, grappling with family loyalty and emotional conflicts.

Essentially, *Kaala Sona* is a revenge tale. The narrative follows a young man's quest to avenge his father's murder, an oft-repeated and all-too-familiar theme in Bollywood action movies. However, director Ravikant Nagaich, known for his espionage thrillers such as *Farz* (1967) and *Keemat* (1973), offers a novel perspective by setting the drama within the realm of illicit poppy farming and the opium trade. This thematic twist propels *Kaala Sona* beyond a typical action-revenge story, infusing it with a raised sense of lawlessness. The film crafts an Indian Wild West, populated with outlaws, rugged landscapes and a dark world of crime as well as a visually and thematically mesmerizing setting.

One of the film's most memorable elements is its villain, Poppy Singh, who is brought to life with vivacious flair by Prem Chopra. His name playfully alludes to his trade, but it is Chopra's lively and almost deliberately over-the-top theatrical performance that makes Singh such an unforgettable villain. He is both intimidating and delightfully entertaining, and he introduces a layer of dark humour to the film. His flamboyant mannerisms, sharp dialogue delivery and menacing laughter create a villain who revels in his own mischief. In many ways, Prem Chopra's acting is a key factor in *Kaala Sona's* enduring legacy; his Poppy Singh is not just a criminal mastermind but a scene-stealer who provides the necessary effervescence to complement Khan's more restrained and brooding performance.

The film also shines thanks to a robust supporting cast. Parveen Babi, at the height of her fame, infuses glamour and modernity into the film. Rather than fitting the traditional damsel-in-distress mould, she embodies a heroine with both style and substance and who also asserts herself strongly in the male-dominated world of *Kaala Sona*. Danny Denzongpa, another stalwart of Hindi cinema, lends his signature intensity to his role. His screen presence guarantees that the narrative possesses deeper layers beyond the hero-villain dynamic.

A defining feature of *Kaala Sona* is its music, composed by the brilliant R.D. Burman. His soundtrack skilfully mixes western-inspired elements with classic Bollywood sounds and tropes, ensuring that while *Kaala Sona* draws heavily from spaghetti westerns in its aesthetics and narrative, its heart remains unmistakably Indian. The film's songs are infused with Burman's signature energy and creativity, making the film even more alluring. Numbers like '*Tak Jhoom Nacho*', '*Koi Aaya*' and '*Ek Baar Jaane Na*' gained widespread popularity at the film's release, but the standout track was undoubtedly '*Sunn Sunn Kasam Se*'. This duet, featuring Danny Denzongpa and Asha Bhosle, not only became the highest-charting song of the soundtrack but also marked Danny's debut as a playback singer. The song remains an intriguing piece of Bollywood trivia, as Danny would later collaborate with Kishore Kumar in the 1978 film *Naya Daur* once again under Burman's musical baton.

Visually, *Kaala Sona* distinguishes itself with its unique aesthetic. The dusty landscapes, rugged backdrops and wide-angle shots (Nagaich's trademark style, used in almost all his films) reflect the look of spaghetti westerns, whereas the flamboyant set pieces and vibrant costumes adhere to Bollywood's grand storytelling. The action sequences are well-crafted and teeming with stylized shootouts, horseback pursuits and dramatic confrontations that heighten the film's entertainment value. Nagaich's direction strikes a balance between intense action and melodramatic emotion, which prevents the film from becoming too serious.

Although *Kaala Sona* may not be the first name that springs to mind when discussing the most iconic Bollywood films of the 1970s, it undoubtedly holds a special place among genre enthusiasts. The film indulges in its excesses – be it in its action, performances or its hilariously entertaining villain. It embodies a quintessential 'guilty pleasure' film that boasts its own style and bravado and unapologetically embraces its over-the-top storytelling. However, to classify *Kaala Sona* solely as a 'guilty pleasure' would undermine its essence – a film that dared to present an experimental and audacious fusion of Hollywood and Bollywood styles.

For fans of spaghetti westerns, Bollywood action adventures or anyone looking for unabashed cinematic joy, *Kaala Sona* offers an exhilarating experience. It showcases Feroz Khan not just as a star but as a creative force who contributed significantly to refreshing the aesthetics of Hindi cinema. Whether enjoyed for its stylish hero, eccentric villain or the catchy soundtrack, *Kaala Sona* remains an underrated commercial gem that merits more attention.

CAST: Feroz Khan, Parveen Babi, Danny, Farida Jalal, Keshto Mukherjee, Helen, Prem Chopra
OTHER CREDITS: Directed by Ravikant Nagaich. Music by R.D. Burman.
RELEASE DATE: 29 July 1975
BOX OFFICE RESULT: Hit
RUNNING TIME: 2 Hours 17 Mins
TRIVIA: The title music of *Kaala Sona* was later used as inspiration to create the song '*Tum Kya Jaano Mohabbat Kya Hai*' from *Hum Kisise Kum Nahin* (1977).

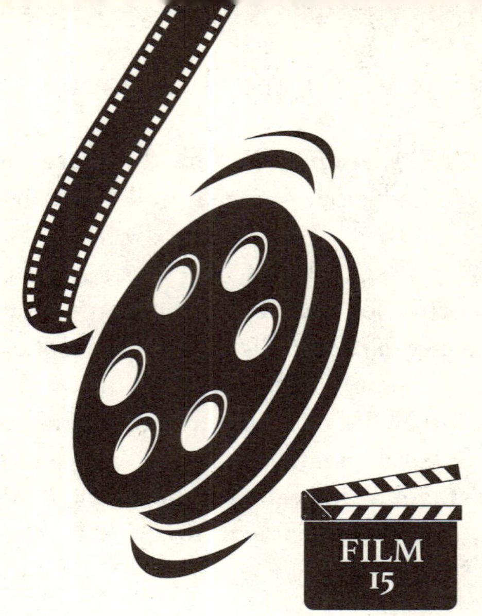

KHEL KHEL MEIN: YOUTHFUL ENTERTAINER WITH MUSIC, MYSTERY AND ROMANCE

Ravi Tandon's *Khel Khel Mein* serves up a delightful blend of youthful romance, catchy music and nail-biting suspense. Now that it marks its fifty-year milestone, the film is a nostalgic nod to the breezy musical suspense films of the 1960s defined by gems like *Teesri Manzil*. Starring Rishi Kapoor, Neetu Singh, Rakesh Roshan, Aruna Irani and Ifteqar, *Khel Khel Mein* perfectly captures the spirit of 1970s' Bollywood by deftly mixing entertainment with a hint of mystery.

The storyline follows a group of college buddies who indulge in playful pranks to keep themselves entertained. What starts off as innocent fun soon morphs into a dramatic situation when their light-hearted antics spiral out of control, leading them into

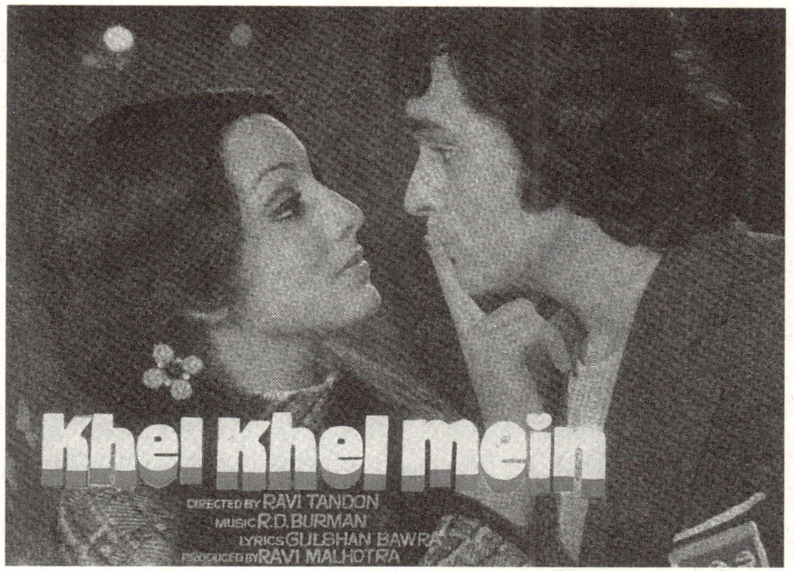

a dangerous web of suspense and unexpected challenges. This blend of easy-going humour and the unforeseen evokes the charm of 1960s suspense films but with a fresh spin. The outcome is a movie that strikes a chord with a broad audience by keeping them entertained and engaged.

Central to *Khel Khel Mein* is the blossoming romance between Ajay (Rishi Kapoor) and Nisha (Neetu Singh). Their authentic on-screen chemistry, impassioned by their real-life romance, adds an extra layer of sincerity to the film. Rishi Kapoor's boyish allure and Neetu Singh's vivaciousness transform them into one of the era's most adored on-screen couples.

The film's romantic scenes are beautifully complemented by its music, which plays a vital role in enriching the emotional essence of the story. The soundtrack, composed by the legendary R.D.

Burman, is a mix of upbeat numbers and soulful ballads, with each contributing to the film's plot progression and enhancing the film's youthful vibe.

The music in *Khel Khel Mein* stands out as one of its most memorable elements. R.D. Burman's compositions, with lyrics written by Anand Bakshi, are both catchy and melodious. Tracks like '*Khullam Khulla Pyar Karenge Hum Dono*', '*Humne Tumko Dekha*', '*Sapna Mera Toot Gaya*' and '*Ek Mein Aur Ek Tu*' became instant hits and continue to be loved to this day.

The title track, '*Khel Khel Mein*' (which appears in the background at crucial moments in the film), is especially noteworthy for its romantic and breezy tone that perfectly encapsulates the film's carefree spirit. The music is masterfully woven into the narrative, which results in amplifying emotional and dramatic moments.

Though *Khel Khel Mein* leans heavily into the realms of romance and music, it also incorporates thrilling elements of suspense. The group's adventures take an unexpected twist when their harmless pranks lead to a cascade of scary situations for them. This twist introduces a layer to the story that keeps the viewer on the edge of their seat without detracting from the film's light-heartedness. The harmonious mix of romance, music and suspense echoes some iconic films of the 1960s; however, *Khel Khel Mein* carved out its unique appeal. This balance of various elements showcases Ravi Tandon's competent direction and the strong foundations of its screenplay, which ensures that the film flows at a lively pace. The cinematography, particularly the picturesque shots of Srinagar, makes the film visually stunning, clearly highlighting Tandon's talent as a film-maker. Fifty years later, *Khel Khel Mein* is fondly remembered as a film that celebrated youth, friendship and love. Its engaging narrative and unforgettable music as well as the cast's exceptional performances secured its place in the hearts of audiences. The film's knack for invoking nostalgia for a past era while remaining thoroughly entertaining attests to its lasting charm.

At a time when cinema often gravitated towards intricate plots and explosive action to enthral audiences, *Khel Khel Mein* reminds us of the joy found in simplicity and the potency of heartfelt stories.

As *Khel Khel Mein* reaches its fifty-year milestone, it has become a symbol of the golden age of Bollywood. The film's celebration of youth, its catchy music by R.D. Burman, and the chemistry between its leads contribute to its timelessness. For those who grew up in the 1970s, it serves as a nostalgic journey, and for newer viewers, it offers a delightful peek into the charm of classic Bollywood.

CAST: Rishi Kapoor, Neetu Singh, Rakesh Roshan, Aruna Irani, Satyen Kappu, Ifteqar, Dev Kumar
OTHER CREDITS: Directed by Ravi Tandon. Music by R.D. Burman.
RELEASE DATE: 16 May 1975
BOX OFFICE RESULT: Hit
RUNNING TIME: 2 Hours 19 Mins
TRIVIA: The hit song '*Ek Main Aur Ek Tu*' was inspired by a nursery rhyme, 'If You're Happy and You Know, It Clap Your Hands'.

Mithun Chakraborty appears as an extra in one scene of the movie.

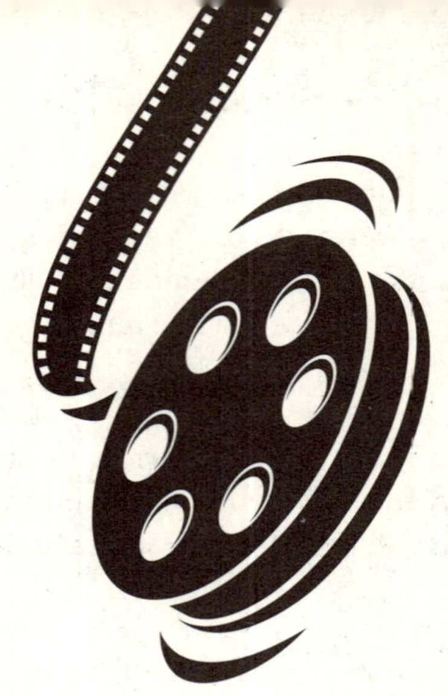

THE IMPACT OF THE 1975 EMERGENCY ON THE HINDI FILM INDUSTRY

The Emergency declared by the then-prime minister Indira Gandhi on 25 June 1975, marked a dark chapter in India's democratic history. For 21 months, the government suspended civil liberties, majorly censored the press and jailed many political opponents. This period had far-reaching impacts on all aspects of Indian society, including the Hindi film industry, which faced unprecedented scrutiny, censorship and repression.

One of the most notable films affected by the Emergency in 1975 was *Sholay*, a landmark Bollywood film. The original ending of *Sholay* was supposed to be the ex-police officer protagonist, Thakur Baldev Singh, exacting personal vengeance by killing the antagonist, Gabbar Singh. However, the government, under its strict censorship regime, mandated a change to this climax. The authorities believed that such a depiction of personal revenge could incite violence and promote vigilante justice, which was deemed unsuitable during a time of heightened political control. As a result, the film-makers were forced to create a less violent, more law-abiding conclusion where the antagonist is captured by the police, aligning the film with the state's emphasis on law and order.

Another significant casualty of the Emergency was the film *Aandhi* (1975), directed by Gulzar. The film featured a woman politician who is estranged from her husband, which led to widespread speculation that the character was modelled after the then-prime minister Indira Gandhi. Despite the film's nuanced portrayal that had no direct similarity with Indira Gandhi's life, the government still perceived it as a threat, fearing it might incite the opposition to diminish Mrs Gandhi's image. It is interesting to note that till the time Emergency was declared, *Aandhi* was running to packed houses for 23 weeks. It is rumoured that Sanjay Gandhi wanted Gulzar to speak on behalf of the Youth Congress on its objectives and plans, an offer that Gulzar politely declined. Consequently, *Aandhi* was banned, becoming a casualty of the regime's intolerance towards any perceived critique or unflattering portrayal of its leaders. It was only after the Emergency ended and the government was ousted that *Aandhi* was re-released and found commercial and critical success, underscoring the arbitrary nature of the censorship it faced.

I.S. Johar's *Nasbandi* (1978) was another film that faced severe backlash from the government. This satirical film critiqued the government's policy of forced sterilizations, which was an abhorrent cornerstone of the Emergency's population control measures. *Nasbandi* used humour and caricature to expose the draconian measures and human rights abuses carried out under this policy. The film featured lookalikes of prominent Hindi film stars, which further angered the establishment. As a result, *Nasbandi* was banned, and Johar faced significant personal and professional risks.

Some film-makers decided to tweak their storylines and treatment of films, fearing the wrath of the administration during this period. Launched in 1976, fresh from the success of *Sholay*, the film *Ram Balram* starred the same lead pair of Dharmendra and Amitabh Bachchan with the intention of shooting a fun film laden with action and comedy. The film was to depict the unique partnership of a thief and a cop who were hand-in-glove to commit frauds and schemes to make money. The writers however decided to change the mood of the film to that of a regular masala movie during the Emergency due to fears that showing a police officer in such a light might make the administration create problems for the film.

The most egregious example of censorship was perhaps the case of *Kissa Kursi Ka* (1977), directed by Amrit Nahata. This film was a scathing satire on the corruption and nepotism rampant in the government. Before its release, the film was submitted to the censor board, as is required. However, the original prints of the film were seized and destroyed by government operatives in an act that epitomized the extreme measures taken to stifle dissent. The destruction of *Kissa Kursi Ka* was a stark reminder of the lengths to which the government would go to suppress critical narratives and control the flow of information. The entire film was remade again in 1978, but the damage was already done by then.

Another important development during the Emergency was the banning of the songs of the most beloved and leading playback singer of the industry, Kishore Kumar. Kishore had refused to perform for free at a Congress rally where a whole lot of film personalities were also performing. The government wanted the industry's help in promoting Mrs Gandhi's 20-point programme for development. Kishore's refusal irked the government authorities, especially the then–information-and-broadcast minister V.C. Shukla and joint secretary C.B. Jain, and his songs were promptly banned from being broadcast on All India Radio. Any song that featured Kishore Kumar was excluded from AIR during that period. It was only after Kishore wrote a letter to the government and then the subsequent falling of the government that the ban was lifted.

Actors like Dev Anand, Manoj Kumar and Amol Palekar too were harassed by Congress activists for their refusal to speak on behalf of the Youth Congress on Sanjay Gandhi's request. Dev Anand in particular was so upset by the happenings during Emergency that he decided to form his own political party, the National Party of India, which also included eminent personalities like Vijaylakshmi Pandit (the sister of Jawaharlal Nehru) and Nani Palkhiwala. Dev, however, had to disband his party after he failed to gather sufficient funds for running it and getting representatives to stand for elections.

The Emergency period was akin to a dark age for the Hindi film industry. Film-makers were unfairly forced to navigate an environment of intense scrutiny with curtailed artistic expression, and any deviation from state-approved narratives could lead to severe consequences. This censorship stifled creativity and prevented important social and political issues from being explored in cinema.

However, the resilience of the industry and its practitioners eventually triumphed. Once the Emergency was lifted, banned films were re-released and received widespread acclaim, illuminating the public's appetite for diverse and critical viewpoints. The legacy of this period serves as a potent reminder of the power of cinema to challenge authority and reflect societal truths as well as the importance of safeguarding artistic freedom from authoritarian forces.

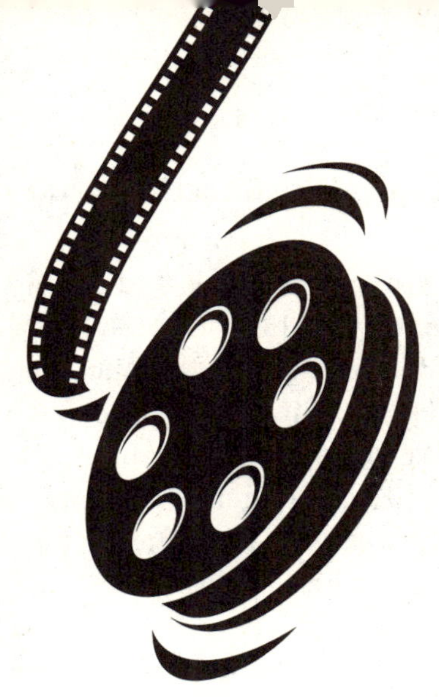

THE TOP MALE STARS OF BOLLYWOOD IN 1975: A YEAR OF TRANSITION AND TRANSFORMATION

THE LEADING MEN

The year 1975 marked a critical shift in Bollywood's star power and audience preferences. While the decade had begun with the Rajesh Khanna wave in the early 1970s, by the mid-1970s, the industry began undergoing a dynamic change. A mix of established superstars, rising challengers and fresh young faces shaped the cinematic landscape of this year. Among them, Rajesh Khanna, Dharmendra, Amitabh Bachchan and Dev Anand remained the leading names, while newer stars like Rishi Kapoor also made their presence felt.

Rajesh Khanna: The Fading Reign of the First Superstar

Rajesh Khanna, the man who had once been the undisputed king of Bollywood, saw his dominance begin to wane by 1975. His films had started flopping between 1972 and 1973, a shocking turn of events for someone who had once delivered 17 consecutive solo super-hits. While he was still a formidable star, the magic that had once captivated audiences was no longer as potent. His only major release in 1975, *Prem Kahani*, was a significant film, but it did not match the hysteria generated by his earlier hits. Nevertheless, his acting prowess and loyal fan base ensured that he remained one of the top names in the industry, even as newer stars started taking over.

Dharmendra: The Evergreen Action Hero

One of the few actors who had managed to hold his ground even during Rajesh Khanna's peak years was Dharmendra. He continued his winning streak in 1975 with multiple successful films, proving his versatility and mass appeal. His biggest triumph came in the form of *Sholay*, one of the greatest films ever made in Indian cinema, where his role as Veeru became iconic. Apart from *Sholay*, he also delivered hits like *Pratiggya*, *Chupke Chupke* and *Ek Mahal Ho Sapno Ka*, thus showing his ability to balance action-packed roles with comedy and romance. His consistent success at the box-office made him one of the most bankable stars of the era, especially through movies in which he was paired with Hema Malini.

Amitabh Bachchan: The Rise of the Angry Young Man

If there was one actor who truly defined 1975, it was Amitabh Bachchan. From playing second fiddle to Rajesh Khanna in *Anand* (1971), Bachchan had slowly built his reputation with films like *Zanjeer* (1973), which introduced the angry young man archetype. In 1975, he firmly established his position as Bollywood's biggest star with an unmatched lineup of hits. *Sholay* saw him deliver a career-defining performance as Jai, while *Deewaar* showcased his intense and brooding persona that was deeply loved by audiences. He also balanced these with subtle-yet-powerful performances in *Mili* and *Chupke Chupke*, proving his range even more. *Faraar* and *Zameer* further added to his impressive year. By the end of 1975, it was clear that Amitabh Bachchan was the new numero uno of Bollywood.

Dev Anand: The Veteran Who Refused to Fade

Dev Anand, one of the legendary stars from the 1950s and 1960s, had seen ups and downs in the early 1970s. While *Johnny Mera Naam* (1970) had been a massive hit, his banner Navketan had struggled with flops like *Ishk Ishk Ishk* (1974). However, he made a strong comeback in 1975 with *Warrant*, a film that reaffirmed his status as a crowd-puller. Despite the changing trends, Dev Anand's uniquely charismatic acting style and ability to reinvent himself kept him relevant, and he continued to be counted among the top stars of the industry.

Rishi Kapoor: The Young Heartthrob

While the leading men of the 1970s were largely in their thirties and forties, Rishi Kapoor emerged as the face of the younger generation. Having debuted as a teenaged romantic hero in *Bobby* (1973), he continued his success with *Khel Khel Mein* and *Rafoo Chakkar* in 1975. Both films, co-starring Neetu Singh, were youthful romances that appealed to the teenaged crowds, proving that Bollywood was gradually moving on from older stars to cast younger heroes. While he was not yet a contender for the top spot, his growing popularity hinted at the changing tastes of the audience.

OTHER NOTABLE STARS OF 1975

Beyond the leading men, several other actors delivered notable performances and hits in 1975.

Vinod Khanna and Sanjeev Kumar continued to shine in supporting but significant roles. Sanjeev Kumar, in particular, enjoyed immense success with *Sholay*, wherein his portrayal of Thakur was unforgettable. Manoj Kumar, known for his patriotic films, remained relevant with the super-hit *Sanyasi*. Shashi Kapoor, though overshadowed by his more dominant contemporaries, had a steady career with films where he often played the suave, sophisticated hero. His solo hero film *Chori Mera Kaam* was a huge feather in his cap.

THE YEAR THAT CHANGED BOLLYWOOD

The year 1975 was a defining year in Bollywood's history that witnessed the consolidation of Amitabh Bachchan as the new superstar and the decline of Rajesh Khanna's dominance. Dharmendra and Dev Anand proved their staying power, and Rishi Kapoor signalled the arrival of actors from a younger generation. The industry was in a state of flux, but this very dynamism made the era so exciting. Looking back, 1975 was significant year that shaped the future of Bollywood.

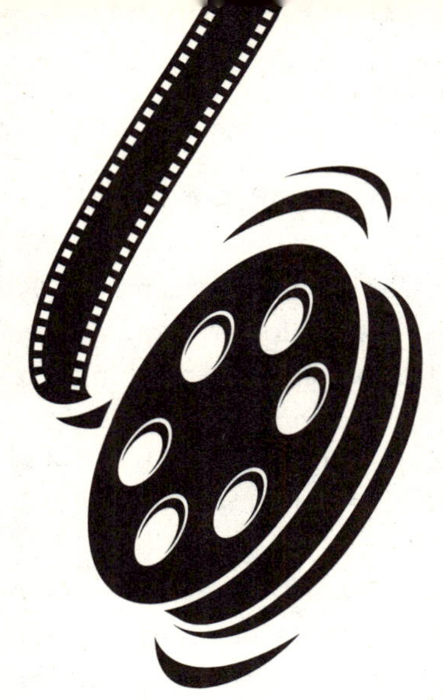

THE LEADING LADIES: A YEAR OF POWERFUL PERFORMANCES AND EVOLVING ROLES

The year 1975 is often remembered as a golden chapter in the history of Bollywood, especially because of the dynamic female performances that redefined the roles of heroines in Hindi cinema. While the industry had traditionally revolved around male superstars, 1975 witnessed a surge of leading ladies who equally contributed to adding depth, versatility and a new energy to the big screen. Foremost among them was Hema Malini, who stood as the undisputed queen of Bollywood during this defining year. Alongside her were other formidable names such as Zeenat Aman, Parveen Babi, Sharmila Tagore and Rekha, along with emerging stars like Neetu Singh and Sulakshana Pandit.

Hema Malini: The Unchallenged Superstar

At the pinnacle of her career, Hema Malini reigned supreme in 1975, delivering a string of box-office hits that reinforced her status as the numero uno heroine of the era. Her performances in films like *Sholay*, *Pratiggya*, *Dharmatma*, *Khushboo* and *Sanyasi* showcased not only her glamour and brilliant screen presence but also her ability to hold her own in films dominated by powerful male leads.

In the cult classic *Sholay*, Hema played the role of Basanti, who is a feisty and talkative *tonga* driver whose vivacity balanced the otherwise intense narrative. Her chemistry with Dharmendra, which had already become a crowd-puller by then, was electric and added a memorable romantic layer to the action-packed drama. *Dharmatma* saw her paired again with Feroz Khan in a more intense but short role, while *Sanyasi* and *Pratiggya* further showed off her versatility, ranging from comedy, drama and action.

Yet it was her role in Gulzar's *Khushboo* that added a deeper dimension to her filmography. As Kusum, Hema portrayed a woman torn between love and moral obligations with a quiet strength and emotional depth that won critical acclaim. In doing so, she proved that she was more than just a glamorous star; she became revered as an actress capable of navigating complex emotional terrain with ease and grace.

Zeenat Aman and Parveen Babi: Modernity and Boldness Redefined

If Hema Malini represented the reigning traditional star, Zeenat Aman and Parveen Babi brought a bold new energy to Bollywood's heroines, being women who were not afraid to challenge the rigid existing norms.

Zeenat's role in *Warrant* may not have been as high-profile as her earlier films, but it reinforced her image as a stylish, urban woman who didn't conform to the docile, demure female archetype of the past. Her screen persona was assertive, independent and sophisticated, which mirrored the changing aspirations of Indian women in the mid-1970s.

On the other hand, Parveen Babi created waves with her portrayal of Anita in Yash Chopra's *Deewaar*. As an independent woman in a live-in relationship with Amitabh Bachchan's character, she brought a quiet boldness to the screen. The iconic scene where she shares a cigarette in bed with him was symbolic of a cultural shift in how women were portrayed – not as accessories to the hero but as real, layered individuals in their own right. Her performance was groundbreaking and signalled the evolving on-screen representation of modern Indian women.

Mumtaz: A Graceful Goodbye

Though Mumtaz had largely stepped away from films after her marriage in 1974, her only release in 1975, *Prem Kahani*, was noteworthy. Despite the film's underwhelming box-office performance, Mumtaz's portrayal of a woman caught between two men (played by Rajesh Khanna and Shashi Kapoor) was poignant yet powerful. Her screen presence remained magnetic, proving she hadn't lost her touch and providing a fitting farewell to an illustrious career.

Neetu Singh: The Fresh Face of Youth

The bubbly and effervescent Neetu Singh was transitioning from her earlier child roles into full-fledged leading ladies, and 1975 marked a significant step in that journey. She starred in two major hits – *Khel Khel Mein* and *Rafoo Chakkar* – both opposite Rishi Kapoor. Their on-screen chemistry was sizzling and full of youthful passion, which easily won over audiences and paved the way for their real-life romance, which would culminate in marriage years later. Neetu's roles reflected the modern, middle-class girl-next-door with vibrance and relatability.

Rekha: The Turning Point

Though still trying to break into mainstream stardom, Rekha finally began to find her footing in 1975. Her performance in R.K. banner's *Dharam Karam* gave her much-needed visibility, while her secondary role in Feroz Khan's *Dharmatma* alongside Hema Malini was also noticed. These roles marked a transition from her earlier B-grade films to more respectable and impactful roles in mainstream movies. This new success set the stage for the powerful actress she would become in the late 1970s and early 1980s.

Sharmila Tagore: The Veteran's Elegance

Already an established actress, Sharmila Tagore continued to deliver impactful performances in 1975. Her comic timing in *Chupke Chupke* opposite Dharmendra was impeccable, while her intense role in *Faraar* brought her gravitas. However, it was Gulzar's *Mausam* that brought her back into critical focus. Playing a dual role – one of a betrayed mother and the other of her foul-mouthed courtesan daughter – Sharmila delivered a deeply moving performance that was both complex and emotionally stirring, thereby reaffirming her status as one of the finest actresses of her generation.

Sulakshana Pandit: A Promising Debut

Finally, Sulakshana Pandit made a notable debut in *Uljhan* opposite the ever-reliable Sanjeev Kumar. A classical beauty with a background in music, she showed promise not just as a singer but also as a capable actress. Her performance was well-received, and while she didn't go on to dominate the screen in later years, her debut remains one of the year's most noteworthy introductions.

Looking back, 1975 was not only a year of male-dominated blockbusters but also a year when the portrayals of Bollywood's heroines evolved. Hema Malini led the charge with a near-perfect blend of glamour, acting prowess and box office clout. Following her, Zeenat Aman and Parveen Babi introduced new-age modernity to female roles, and veterans like Sharmila Tagore and Mumtaz displayed finesse and emotional depth. Moreover, new but rising stars like Neetu Singh and Sulakshana Pandit showed the promise of a new generation of heroines. Together, these actresses helped broaden the scope of what it meant to be a Bollywood leading lady, forever changing the landscape of Hindi cinema.

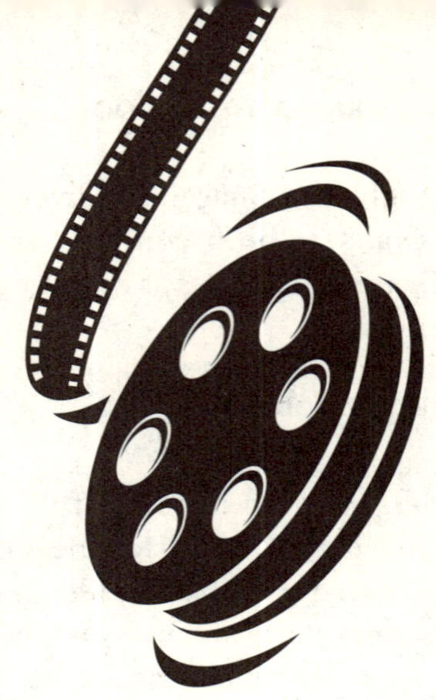

THE LEADING FILM-MAKERS OF BOLLYWOOD IN 1975: A LANDMARK YEAR OF VISION AND VERSATILITY

The year 1975 is often hailed as one of the most trailblazing in the history of Indian cinema. It was a year that not only gave audiences timeless films but also spotlighted an extraordinary roster of film-makers, some of whom left a lasting impact on Bollywood through their distinct styles. From groundbreaking blockbusters to nuanced dramas, directors across the spectrum showcased their creative prowess, some more successfully than others. The top brass during this cinematic revolution included names like Ramesh Sippy, Yash Chopra and Gulzar among many other master craftsmen.

Ramesh Sippy: The Film-Maker of the Year

At just 28 years old, Ramesh Sippy delivered what would go on to become one of the greatest and universally loved movies in Indian cinema – *Sholay*. Although the film had a lukewarm start at the box office, it soon picked up steam and ultimately rewrote the rules of Indian film-making as an all-time blockbuster. Sippy's vision was unprecedented; it was a genre-defining blend of action, emotion, drama and unforgettable characters, all wrapped in an epic format rarely attempted in Hindi cinema until then.

Coming off the successes of *Andaz* and *Seeta Aur Geeta*, both of which hinted at his flair for the portrayal of emotion and comedy, *Sholay* was the ultimate realization of all that promise. This cinematic feat showcased not only his technical brilliance but also his ability to handle ensemble casts, massive set-pieces and intricate emotional arcs. His collaboration with the writer duo Salim–Javed, cinematographer Dwarka Divecha and a cast of megastars resulted in a film that remains evergreen. In many ways, it can be said that 1975 belonged to Ramesh Sippy.

Yash Chopra: The Rise of a Master Storyteller

Already a promising name after stepping out of his brother B.R. Chopra's shadow with *Daag* (1972), Yash Chopra made his grand statement in 1975 with *Deewaar*. A hard-hitting emotional drama about two brothers caught on opposite sides of law and morality, *Deewaar* was a potent story elevated by Salim–Javed's taut script and Chopra's restrained, mature direction.

Chopra handled the film's complex themes – abandonment, class struggle and rebellion – with deftness and sensitivity. His ability to extract layered performances from Amitabh Bachchan, Shashi Kapoor, Nirupa Roy and Parveen Babi further proved his mettle. *Deewaar* not only gave Bollywood one of its most iconic antiheroes but also cemented Yash Chopra's reputation as a director capable of balancing commercial viability with narrative depth. The film was a definitive turning point in his career and marked him as one of the foremost storytellers of his time.

Gulzar: The Prolific Poet of Cinema

In a time when most film-makers considered a single film in a year an achievement, Gulzar turned the notion of quantity versus quality on its head by delivering not one but three remarkable films in 1975 – *Aandhi*, *Mausam* and *Khushboo*. Each film was distinct in tone and theme but carried his unmistakable poetic storytelling, emotional intelligence and socio-political commentary.

Aandhi was a bold and controversial film that drew parallels with the life of the then-prime minister Indira Gandhi. Despite political censorship, the film won critical acclaim for its nuanced portrayal of a woman torn between personal desires and public duty. *Mausam*, released later in the year, showcased Sharmila Tagore in a powerful double role and won accolades for its melancholic and introspective tone and Gulzar's masterful direction. *Khushboo*, a more understated yet moving film, brought out Hema Malini's subtle emotional strength in a story about loss and reconciliation.

With these three films, Gulzar demonstrated that artistry need not be compromised for commercial success. His ability to dive deep into human emotions while maintaining a sensitive-yet-accessible cinematic language made him arguably the most prolific and respected film-maker of 1975.

The Bengali Aesthetic: Shakti Samanta, Basu Chatterjee, Hrishikesh Mukherjee and Pramod Chakravorty

A host of Bengali film-makers also made their mark in 1975 with successful films that combined substance with mass appeal.

Shakti Samanta, known for his flair for music-rich emotional dramas, continued to remain relevant, while Basu Chatterjee and Hrishikesh Mukherjee ruled the middle cinema space with their light-hearted yet meaningful stories. These directors brought everyday life to the big screen with warmth, wit and gentle irony, thus allowing the audience to see themselves reflected in the film. Samanta's bilingual *Amanush* starring Uttam Kumar turned out to be a huge hit, making it the first real success the Bengali superstar tasted in Bollywood. Hrishikesh Mukherjee's *Chupke Chupke*, a delightful comedy of errors, remains one of the most beloved comedies of all time. With a stellar cast led by Dharmendra and Amitabh Bachchan, the film's clever writing and humorous situations became an instant hit. Pramod Chakravorty, known for commercial entertainers, also found success in 1975 with *Warrant*, proving that film-makers from this school of cinema could balance the tightrope of mass appeal and meaningful storytelling.

The Commercial Craftsmen: Raghunath Jhalani, Ravi Tandon, Brij and Ravikant Nagaich

In the realm of mass entertainers, directors like Raghunath Jhalani, Ravi Tandon, Brij and Ravikant Nagaich delivered solid hits that catered to the mainstream audience's palate.

Jhalani's *Uljhan* was a taut thriller featuring a standout debut performance from Sulakshana Pandit. Ravi Tandon, the father of actress Raveena Tandon, delivered *Khel Khel Mein*, a youthful caper starring the fresh pairing of Rishi Kapoor and Neetu Singh. Brij, known for his slick commercial sensibility, scored highly with *Chori Mera Kaam*, a crime comedy starring Shashi Kapoor and Zeenat Aman. Ravi Nagaich, who had earlier made spy hits like *Farz* (1967), *The Train* (1970) and *Keemat* (1973), delivered a curry-western super-hit with *Kaala Sona*.

These directors might not have been the darlings of movie critics, but they knew the pulse of the audience and delivered consistent successes that kept the wheels of commercial cinema running. This rich tapestry of directorial voices made 1975 a defining year in the evolution of commercial Indian cinema.

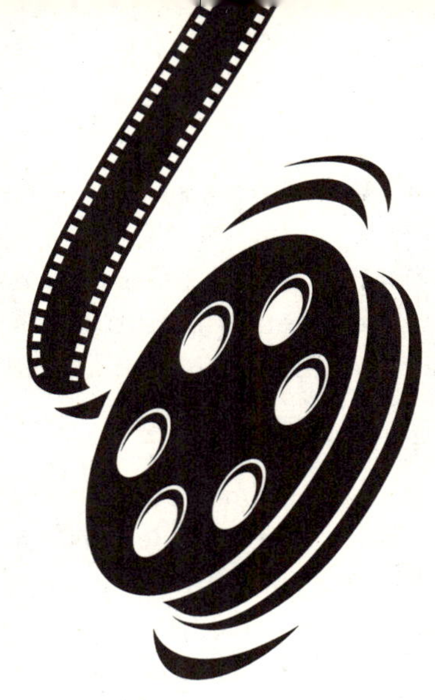

TOP MUSIC COMPOSERS OF BOLLYWOOD IN 1975: A YEAR OF MUSICAL MILESTONES

The year 1975 is often remembered as a high point in the history of Hindi cinema for both its blockbuster films with powerful stories and the exceptionally successful movie soundtracks. The year was a highpoint for composers who made music a balanced combination of melody and innovation. The composers were able to majorly enhance the emotional strength of the movies, despite some of them not performing well commercially. At the forefront of this musical renaissance was R.D. Burman (Pancham), who towered above the rest with his prolific output, genre-defying experimentation and chart-topping success in that single year. Alongside him, stalwarts like Laxmikant–Pyarelal, Kalyanji–Anandji, Ravindra Jain and emerging talent Rajesh Roshan achieved their distinct musical accomplishments. The untimely passing of Madan Mohan also added a sombre layer to the year's music-related timeline.

R.D. Burman: The Undisputed Maestro of 1975

If one name defined the soundscape of 1975, it was R.D. Burman. From thundering blockbusters to offbeat emotional dramas, Pancham delivered hit after hit that established his unmatched versatility and creative brilliance.

In *Sholay*, he composed the pulsating and hypnotic '*Mehbooba Mehbooba*', a song that fused folk, funk and Middle Eastern influences, creating an unforgettable song-and-dance sequence on screen. In *Deewaar*, a film that had little space for music, he sneaked in two Kishore–Asha gems – the peppy '*Keh Doon Tumhe*' and the romantic '*Maine Tujhe Maanga*' – both of which became instant favourites.

Khushboo and *Aandhi*, both directed by Gulzar, revealed Pancham's softer, more introspective side. '*Tere Bina Zindagi Se Koi*' and '*O Majhi Re*' became timeless classics for their soulful emotionality and simplicity. *Dharam Karam*'s music included his homage to vintage musical styles (such as that of R.K. Films' perennial favourite, Shankar Jaikishen) in '*Ek Din Bik Jayega*', sung beautifully by Mukesh, in what would be one of the singer's last standout songs for Raj Kapoor.

In *Khel Khel Mein*, he demonstrated his ability to create youthful and modern music in '*Ek Main Aur Ek Tu*', once again proving he could capture the hearts and imagination of every generation. *Warrant* boasted another crowd-pleaser, '*Ruk Jaana O Jaana*', which helped maintain Dev Anand's cool and stylish on-screen image.

There was no escaping R.D. Burman in 1975 – his music was everywhere, in every genre, in every emotional register. His command over orchestration, ability to fuse Indian melodies with Western genres and instinct for what the narrative demanded made him the defining composer of the year.

Laxmikant–Pyarelal and Kalyanji–Anandji: Reliable Hitmakers

While R.D. Burman reigned supreme, the formidable duo of Laxmikant–Pyarelal continued to be a powerful force in the industry. Their music for *Prem Kahani* was rich and melodic, adding emotional gravitas to the romantic drama. Songs like '*Phool Aahista Phenko*' carried their signature grandeur along with the lyrical beauty of Anand Bakshi, whose pairing with the composer duo was legendary.

Kalyanji–Anandji, too, maintained their stronghold with scores for movies like *Chori Mera Kaam* and *Faraar*. The duo, known for their emotional melodies and rhythmic innovation, stayed relevant even in the rapidly evolving musical climate of the mid-1970s. The title song of *Chori Mera Kaam* and the lilting '*Main Pyasa Tum Saawan*' from *Faraar* enjoyed great popularity that year. This composer duo became known for their consistency in offering traditional melodic structures that resonated with both film-makers and music lovers.

Rajesh Roshan: The Arrival of a New Star

The biggest musical debut of the year, and arguably the most significant new arrival in the Bollywood music scene of 1975, was Rajesh Roshan with his extraordinary score for *Julie*. A film with a relatively offbeat theme, Julie became a massive musical success thanks to Roshan's exquisite compositions. Each and every song from the soundtrack, from the hauntingly beautiful '*Dil Kya Kare*' sung by Kishore Kumar to the romantic 'My Heart Is Beating' in English, became a runaway hit. The melodies were youthful and fresh as well as emotionally deep, immediately establishing Rajesh Roshan as a noteworthy composer. His use of orchestration and ability to deliver traditional melody with a modern approach set in motion the emergence of a new musical era.

Ravindra Jain: Melody Rooted in Simplicity

Composer Ravindra Jain emerged as a formidable musical voice with his work in *Geet Gaata Chal*, a runaway musical hit of the year. A film steeped in Indian traditions and folk ethos, its music was like a breath of fresh air and the proverbial soul of the film. Jain composed songs that were simple yet immensely soulful, such as the film's breezy title track '*Geet Gaata Chal O Saathi*', the emotionally appealing '*Shyam Teri Bansi*' and more, which pulled at the heartstrings of viewers and became emblematic of his style. Jain's music was rooted in the soil – gentle and sincere – and 1975 saw him move closer to the mainstream with enormous grace and impact. He was carving out an individual space where spirituality, romance and innocence coexisted in perfect harmony.

Bappi Lahiri: In the Big League

The young, up-and-coming Bappi Lahiri made his presence felt big time with the music of *Zakhmee*. Each and every song from the film proved to be immensely popular with the listeners and catapulted young Lahiri to the big league. His music in *Chalte Chalte* in the next year would cement his place in the industry, but *Zakhmee* remained an important milestone in his career journey.

Shankar (of Shankar–Jaikishan): The Last Flicker of a Glorious Era

Though past his prime following the passing of Jaikishan, Shankar continued composing under the banner of Shankar–Jaikishan and delivered a commercially successful soundtrack for *Sanyasi.* While the music did not match the brilliance of his earlier years, the fact that it resonated with the masses pointed to the enduring charm of his melodic instincts. It was a final curtain call for the style that had once dominated Hindi film music.

Madan Mohan: A Poignant Farewell

The untimely demise of Madan Mohan in 1975 resulted in a sense of gloom to the year's musical scene. His haunting compositions for *Mausam*, completed before his death, gained even more emotional weight in the context of his passing. Songs like '*Dil Dhoondta Hai*' and '*Ruke Ruke Se Kadam*' carried a delicate sadness in the maestro's signature ghazal-style and classical influences. *Mausam* became a fitting swansong, a reminder of Madan Mohan's immense talent and his ability to touch the soul with his compositions. His loss was felt deeply across the industry and by music lovers alike.

Together these composers made 1975 not just a great year for films but a landmark moment in Hindi film music.

The Singers: Dominance of the Usual Suspects

Amongst the popular singers of that age, Lata Mangeshkar and Asha Bhosle continued their dominance. With songs like

'*Yeh Raatein Nayi Purani*' (*Julie*), '*Maine Kaha Phoolon Se*' (*Mili*), '*Rukey Rukey Se Qadm*' (*Mausam*), '*Aao Tumhe Chaand Pe Le Jaaye*' (*Zakhmee*) and '*Do Naino Mein Aansoo Bhare Hain*' (*Khushboo*), Lata enjoyed one more year of chart-toppers in varied genres. Asha too made her mark with gems like '*Sapna Mera Toot Gaya*' (*Khel Khel Mein*), '*Jaaneman Jaaneman*' (*Chhoti Si Baat*), '*Sunn Sunn Kasam Se*' (*Kaala Sona*) and '*Bechara Dil Kya Kare*' (*Khushboo*). New and younger singers like Preeti Sagar and Sulakshana Pandit were also able to accomplish success with a couple of hit songs; however, despite their immense talent, they were in no position to dismantle the stranglehold the Mangeshkar sisters had on female playback singing. The year 1975 was yet another year which belonged to them.

Amongst the male singers, it was Kishore Kumar's era all the way. Be it the melancholic '*Dil Aisa Kisine Mera Toda*' (*Amanush*), the zestful '*Chori Mera Kaam*' (*Chori Mera Kaam*), the emotional '*Main Pyasa Tum Saawan*' (*Faraar*), the romantic '*Dil Kya Kare*' (*Julie*), the energetic '*Zakhmee Dilon Ka*' (*Zakhmee*) or the sombre '*Tum Bhi Chalo*' (*Zameer*), Kishore was the topmost choice for playback singing for male stars. Stalwarts like Mohammad Rafi and Mukesh took a backseat this year, as Kumar yodelled his way to the top. A lesser-known singer, Jaspal Singh, had a huge hit with his rendition of some lovely songs in Ravindra Jain's *Geet Gaata Chal*, owing to the freshness in his voice and his uninhibited singing style. But just like the dominance of the sisters in the female playback singers, Kishore Kumar remained the numero uno amongst the male singers that year.

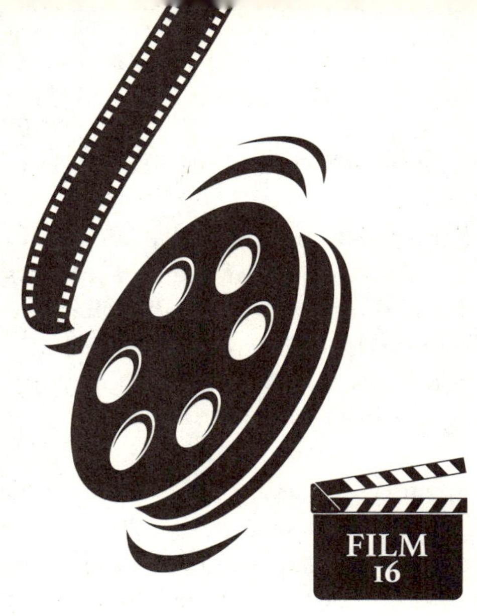

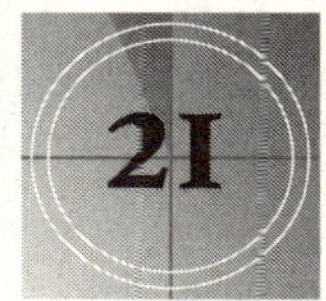

KHUSHBOO: A STUDY IN SUBTLE STRENGTH AND HUMAN EMOTIONS

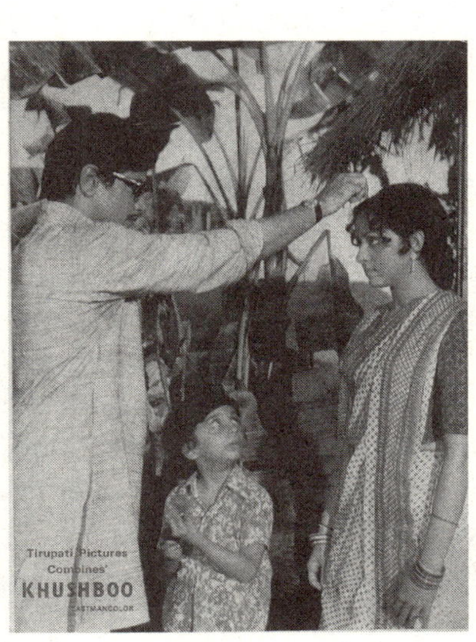

Gulzar's *Khushboo* remains a quiet yet powerful testament to his unique storytelling style – one that emphasizes emotional depth, human relationships and strong female protagonists. Based on *Pandit Moshai*, a novel by Bengali literary giant Sarat Chandra Chatterjee, *Khushboo* is a film that moves away from the typical Bollywood melodrama and commercial trappings, instead becoming an understated and greatly affecting narrative.

Despite featuring two of the most commercially successful stars of the time, Jeetendra and Hema Malini, the film subverts audience expectations by casting them in roles that are diametrically opposite to their established screen images. Under Gulzar's sensitive direction, *Khushboo* unfolds as a gentle, lyrical exploration of love, fate, dignity and resilience.

At its core, *Khushboo* is the story of Kusum (Hema Malini), a woman of quiet strength and self-respect, and Dr Brindavan (Jeetendra), whose life takes an unexpected course due to circumstances beyond his control. The two were married to each other as children, but fate separates them when Brindavan's family moves away. Years later, when he returns as a doctor, he meets Kusum again, who is now an independent woman living with her brother. Despite their childhood engagement, Kusum refuses to be bound by expectations from society and does not immediately accept Brindavan back into her life.

Unlike the conventional love stories of the era, *Khushboo* does not rely on dramatic confrontations or exaggerated emotions. Instead, it portrays the journey of two individuals navigating love with maturity and self-awareness. Kusum, though deeply in love with Brindavan, refuses to compromise on her self-respect, making her one of Gulzar's most compelling heroines.

The film delicately weaves themes of destiny and choice and demonstrates how human relationships are shaped by both external circumstances and personal convictions. There are no villains or overt antagonists in *Khushboo*, only life and its unpredictable turns.

Hema Malini, best known for her glamorous and bubbly roles in commercial cinema, delivers one of the finest performances of her career in *Khushboo*. Kusum is not a rebellious, outspoken feminist; instead, she embodies quiet defiance, refusing to be reduced to a mere pawn in the expectations of a patriarchal society. She does not wail over lost love or beg for validation but rather asserts her dignity in a way that feels natural and relatable.

Her portrayal of Kusum is layered – she is caring but not submissive, in love but not desperate. When Brindavan returns, she does not immediately embrace him, nor does she express resentment. Instead, she remains composed, her strength lying in her ability to wait and choose love on her terms. Gulzar's treatment of her character ensures that her resilience is not dramatized but organically embedded in her very being.

Even now, Kusum's character remains a significant milestone in the portrayal of strong women in Hindi cinema. She represents a kind of feminism that is not in-your-face or overtly radical but deeply personal and empowering.

Jeetendra, often associated with high-energy dance numbers and commercial masala films, surprised audiences with his restrained and sensitive portrayal of Brindavan. He plays the character with a dignified composedness, a stark contrast to his usual flamboyant characters. Brindavan is not a domineering hero or a self-sacrificing lover. He is simply a man caught in the crosscurrents of fate and duty. He respects Kusum's choices, never forcing his love upon her, which helps him gradually and patiently earn his way back into her life. Jeetendra's performance in Khushboo proves that, when given the right role and direction, he was capable of nuanced acting quite different from his commercial image.

Gulzar's signature direction style permeates *Khushboo*, defined by his restraint and emotional intelligence. Unlike the many melodramatic films of the era, *Khushboo* relies solely on the characters' unspoken words, exchanged glances and shared silences. The film's dialogues flow naturally, never feeling forced or theatrical.

The movie's setting also plays a vital role in shaping its tone. Shot against the backdrop of rural India, *Khushboo* exudes an earthy charm that enhances its realism. The landscape, much like the characters, is also simple yet profound.

A Gulzar film is incomplete without a phenomenal soundtrack, and *Khushboo* is no exception. R.D. Burman, in yet another magnificent collaboration with the director, delivers a musical score that seamlessly blends with the film's mood and emotions. Songs like '*Bechara Dil Kya Kare*', '*Ghar Jayegi Tar Jayegi*', '*O Majhi Re*' and '*Do Naino Mein Aansoo Bhare Hain*' are highly revered and enjoyed with nostalgic fondness even today, proving that R.D. Burman's musical genius extended far beyond peppy dance numbers. His ability to compose music that blends seamlessly with a film's storyline remains unmatched.

Even after five decades, *Khushboo* remains relevant not just for its strong female lead but for its deeply humane story. Unlike many feminist portrayals in cinema that rely on overt rebellion, Kusum's stoic strength lies in her refusal to be a victim. She does not fight the system with grand speeches but with small, personal acts of rebellion.

The film also stands as a shining example of how commercial actors can deliver more subdued performances when guided by a director who understands their potential. Both Jeetendra and Hema Malini stepped outside their comfort zones for the movie, a gamble that ultimately paid off for both.

In a decade dominated by action-packed entertainers and dramatic love stories, *Khushboo* stands apart as a film that celebrates patience, resilience and the power of understated emotions. It is a love story not driven by passion or tragedy but by understanding and self-respect. Gulzar's ability to skilfully direct strong women characters without clichés makes *Khushboo* a timeless classic. For those who appreciate cinema that touches the heart without overwhelming the senses, *Khushboo* is just the perfect film to experience.

CAST: Jeetendra, Hema Malini, Asrani, Durga Khote, Farida Jalal, Master Raju, Sharmila Tagore
OTHER CREDITS: Directed by Gulzar. Written by Gulzar based on Sarat Chandra Chatterjee's *Pandit Moshai*. Music by R.D. Burman.
RELEASE DATE: 8 May 1975
BOX OFFICE RESULT: Hit
RUNNING TIME: 2 Hours 13 Mins
TRIVIA: Sharmila Tagore's credit as a 'special appearance' comes in at a strange place during the title credits – in between Gulzar as dialogue writer and R.D. Burman as music director.

R.D. Burman had composed a song for the film sung by Kishore Kumar, '*Mujhko Yun Hi Udaas Rehne Do*'. The song, however, was excluded from the film and its soundtrack record, mainly because there was no situation in the film where it would be relevant.

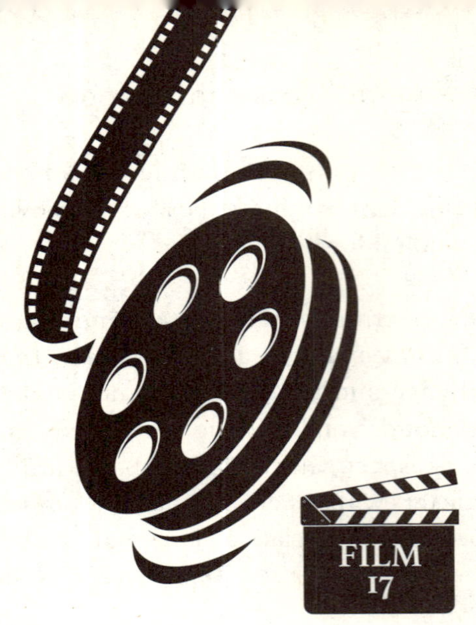

MAUSAM: A WISTFUL TALE OF LOVE AND REDEMPTION

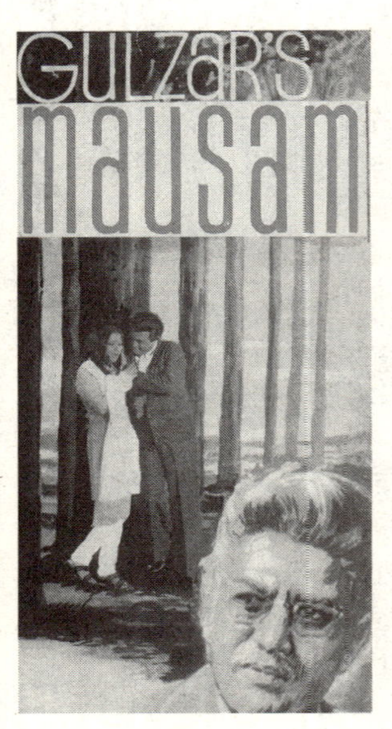

Gulzar's film *Mausam* is a perfect example of skilfully made adaptations in Bollywood, taking its inspiration from A.J. Cronin's novel *The Judas Tree* and shaping it into an Indian narrative. The film explores themes of love, loss, redemption and the passage of time, all woven together with Gulzar's characteristic sensitivity and poetic finesse. Anchored by powerhouse performances from Sanjeev Kumar and Sharmila Tagore, *Mausam* remains a cinematic masterpiece that effectively balances emotional

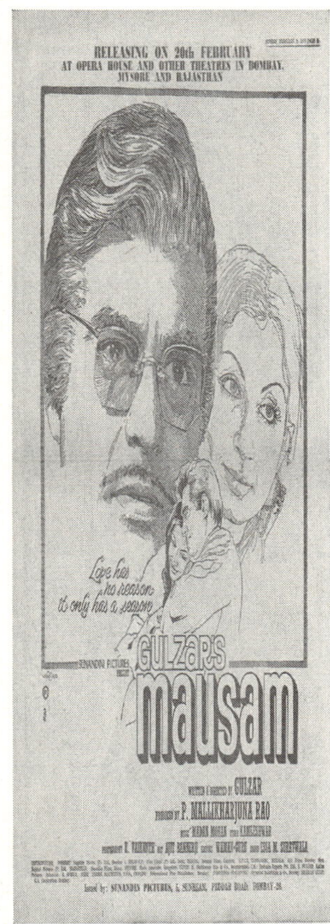

depth with a refined aesthetic.

Mausam tells the story of Dr Amarnath Gill (Sanjeev Kumar), who returns to the hill station Darjeeling after many years, only to confront the ghosts of his past. Although his long-lost love Chanda (Sharmila Tagore) has passed away, he finds her daughter Kajli (also played by Tagore), who grew up in dire circumstances that propel her into sex work at a brothel. The film follows Amarnath's attempts at redemption as he tries to rescue Kajli from her life of hardship.

Gulzar's screenplay masterfully Indianizes the original novel, making it more palatable to Indian sensibilities. While *The Judas Tree* is a stark exploration of guilt and self-recrimination, *Mausam* introduces a nuanced emotional arc with themes of duty, atonement and surrogate fatherhood. Unlike the harsher, more cynical tone of the novel, Gulzar infuses the story with hope and humanism, making Amarnath's redemption journey feel deeply personal and affecting.

The film's success hinges significantly on its performances. Sanjeev Kumar, in the role of the remorseful Amarnath, delivers a performance of great restraint and maturity. His portrayal of a man burdened by regret, trying to make amends in whatever way possible, fills the movie with emotional substance. However, it is Sharmila Tagore who truly astounds with her double role as the demure, innocent Chanda and the brash, wounded Kajli. The contrast between the two roles is striking, and Tagore's ability to switch between them with ease demonstrated her remarkable range. Kajli's rough edges, crass mannerisms, defiance and ultimately vulnerability make her one of the most memorable characters in Hindi cinema of that time.

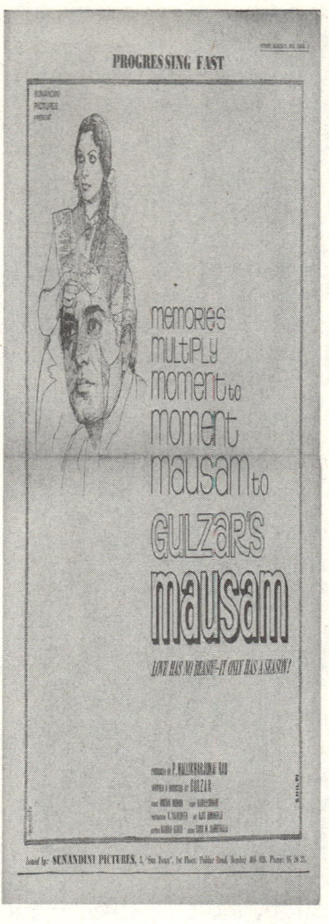

Besides the exceptional performances of its leads, *Mausam* is further elevated by Gulzar's refined direction. His handling of a potentially controversial subject is commendable as he avoids melodrama and infuses the film with subtlety and restraint. The film never sensationalizes Kajli's profession; instead, it focuses on her personhood, allowing the audience to empathize with her plight. The film's narrative progression is patient, enabling moments of quiet reflection that eventually pay off.

Another key factor in the film's appeal is Madan Mohan's exquisite soundtrack. The hauntingly beautiful '*Dil Dhoondta*

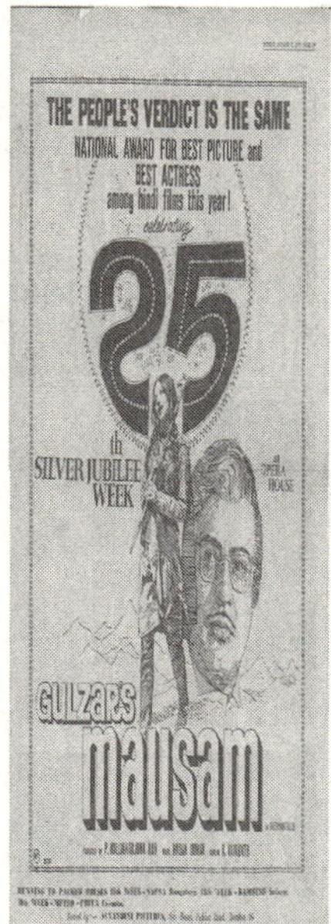

Hai' rendered in two varying versions, one contemplative and the other upbeat, perfectly complements the film's wistful mood. '*Chhadi Re Chhadi*' provides a rare moment of levity, while '*Rukey Rukey Se Qadam*' adds to the movie's melancholic undertones, efficiently enhancing the film's emotional impact.

Despite its bold premise, *Mausam* resonated deeply with audiences largely due to Gulzar's mature and sensitive handling of the subject. His ability to explore complex human emotions without resorting to overt sentimentality is what makes the film a highly revered classic.

CAST: Sanjeev Kumar, Sharmila Tagore, Om Shivpuri, Dina Pathak, Satyen Kappu, C.S. Dubey
OTHER CREDITS: Directed by Gulzar. Music by Madan Mohan.
RELEASE DATE: 29 December 1975
BOX OFFICE RESULT: Average
RUNNING TIME: 2 Hours 36 Mins
TRIVIA: Sharmila Tagore won a National Award for her dual roles of Chanda and Kajli.

Mausam was the last score by Madan Mohan before his death in July 1975.

Salil Chowdhury composed the background score for *Mausam*.

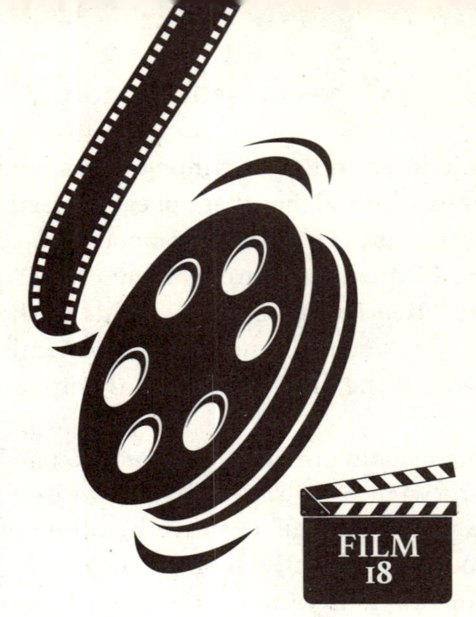

MILI: A BRILLIANT DEPICTION OF HUMAN RELATIONSHIPS AND EMOTIONS

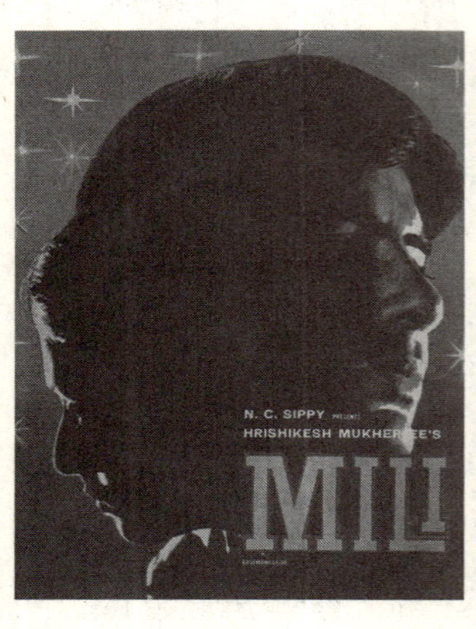

Hrishikesh Mukherjee's *Mili* is an emotionally charged film that masterfully blends romance, melancholy and human resilience and stars Jaya Bhaduri, Amitabh Bachchan and Ashok Kumar. The film is a poignant exploration of love, personal transformation and the impermanence of life. Mukherjee, known for his sensitive storytelling and emotionally immersive narratives, presents a deep human drama in which joy and sorrow coexist seamlessly.

At its heart, *Mili* revolves around the titular character – a young woman whose presence brings warmth and happiness to those around her. Shekhar, played by Amitabh Bachchan, is a bitter, cynical and reclusive alcoholic who moves into the housing complex where Mili lives. While initially indifferent to her infectious energy, Shekhar gradually softens under her influence. His transformation from a misanthropic loner to a caring and compassionate man forms a significant emotional arc in the film. The love story that unfolds between Mili and Shekhar is not merely romantic but symbolic of emotional healing; Mili rescues Shekhar from his inner darkness, even as she battles with her own mortality.

The film takes a tragic turn when Mili is diagnosed with an incurable disease. However, in a departure from conventional melodrama, Mukherjee does not allow Mili to descend into an overtly tragic character. Instead, he maintains a delicate balance between optimism and sorrow. Shekhar, realizing his love for Mili, decides to marry her and take her to Switzerland for treatment.

The film ends on an ambiguous note, as whether Mili survives or not is left open to interpretation. This ending, though uncertain, aligns perfectly with Mukherjee's signature storytelling style, which emphasizes human emotions over definitive conclusions. Jaya Bhaduri's portrayal of Mili is nothing short of extraordinary.

Her transition from a bubbly and vivacious young woman to a bedridden patient struggling with despair is portrayed with much sensitivity. Bhaduri's ability to convey a varying range of emotions, such as joy, vulnerability and eventual resignation, makes Mili an unforgettable character. She does not portray Mili as a tragic figure seeking sympathy but as an embodiment of life itself, full of warmth and love as well as quiet courage.

Amitabh Bachchan, in one of his finest performances, complements Bhaduri's Mili with his nuanced portrayal of Shekhar. His character arc from a man burdened with cynicism and self-destruction to one capable of unconditional love is one of the most compelling aspects of the film. His restrained performance, devoid of his usual flamboyance, allows viewers to clearly perceive the vulnerability behind his tough exterior.

Ashok Kumar, as Mili's loving father, is a constant pillar of strength for her, which adds another layer of emotional depth in the way he deals with his daughter's illness.

Hrishikesh Mukherjee had previously explored the theme of an ailing protagonist in *Anand* (1971), but Mili is strikingly different in both tone and character portrayal. *Anand* features a protagonist who, despite knowing that he is dying, remains an unwavering optimist who spreads joy and laughter until his last breath; he refuses to be defeated by his fate and continues to live life on his own terms.

On the other hand, Mili undergoes the exact opposite life trajectory. At the movie's start, Mili is a lively and cheerful girl, but after her illness is diagnosed, she becomes a shadow of her former self. Unlike Anand, who remains a symbol of unyielding positivity, Mili struggles with despair and weakness. This contrast makes Mili a more relatable character, as she reacts to her illness in a manner that feels real and human. Instead of presenting her as a character who defies fate with undying optimism, Mukherjee makes Mili someone who gradually surrenders to her condition but continues to affect those around her in meaningful ways. The emotional depth of *Mili* is also heightened by its focus on relationships. While *Anand* was primarily about friendship, *Mili* is a film about love, both romantic and familial. The bond between

Mili and Shekhar, as well as her relationship with her father, provides the film with a much-needed emotional backbone.

No discussion of *Mili* would be complete without acknowledging the film's delightful music. The songs composed by the legendary S.D. Burman are not merely musical interludes but an extension of the film's mood and story.

Two songs stand out in particular: '*Badi Sooni Socni Hai*' and '*Aaye Tum Yaad Mujhe*', both sung by Kishore Kumar. '*Badi Sooni Sooni Hai*' is a melancholic masterpiece that conveys the deep loneliness and pain of Shekhar as he grapples with bitterness against his life. '*Aaye Tum Yaad Mujhe*' is a nostalgic melody that evokes a sense of longing and past happiness. The use of music in *Mili* ensures that the film's emotions linger with the audience long after it ends. *Mili* was S.D. Burman's final full-fledged soundtrack before his passing.

One of the most debated aspects of *Mili* is its ending. Mukherjee deliberately chooses not to provide a clear resolution to whether Mili survives or succumbs to her illness. While some may find this ambiguity frustrating, while others project their own hopeful optimism for Mili's survival, it is precisely this open-ended conclusion that makes *Mili* such a remarkable film.

Had the film ended with Mili's death, it would have become a conventional tragedy. Moreover, had it ended with a miraculous recovery, the ending might have seemed unrealistic. Instead, Mukherjee gives us a hopeful but uncertain conclusion, just like life itself. The audience is left with the possibility of survival, but also the acceptance of fate.

For a film-maker who specialized in middle-of-the-road cinema, referring to films that were neither overly dramatic nor purely commercial, this ending was a novel but fitting choice. Mukherjee understood that life does not always provide clear answers, and neither should cinema.

Decades later, *Mili* remains one of Hrishikesh Mukherjee's most heart-wrenching films. Jaya Bhaduri delivers one of her career-best performances, while Amitabh Bachchan brings a depth and vulnerability to his character that was rarely seen in his previous films.

Mukherjee's ability to create deeply human characters combined with S.D. Burman's evocative music ensures that *Mili* remains a deeply moving cinematic experience.

For those who appreciate cinema that tugs at the heartstrings, *Mili* is an experience that serves as a reminder of the fragility of life, but also of the oft-fleeting beauty that exists within it.

CAST: Amitabh Bachchan, Jaya Bhaduri, Ashok Kumar, Aruna Irani
OTHER CREDITS: Directed by Hrishikesh Mukherjee. Written by Bimal Datta, Rahi Masoom Reza. Music by S.D. Burman.
RELEASE DATE: 20 June 1975
BOX OFFICE RESULT: Hit
RUNNING TIME: 2 Hours 30 Mins
TRIVIA: Music director S.D. Burman passed away while *Mili* was still being made. Following his death, R.D. Burman completed the recording of the song '*Badi Sooni Sooni Hai*'. He was credited with a 'grateful acknowledgement' at the start of the film.

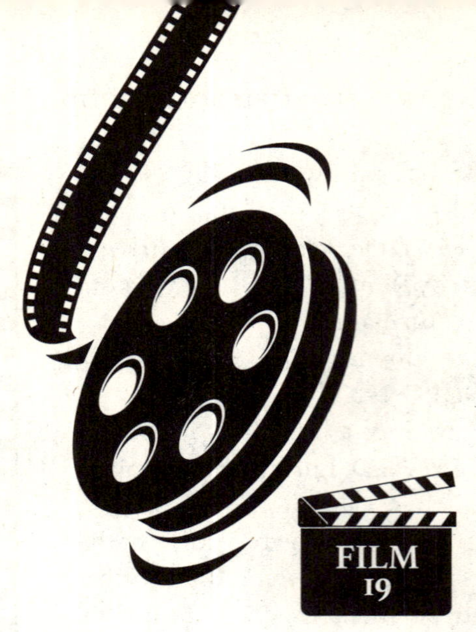

THE UNSETTLING TIMELESSNESS OF *NISHANT*: AN UNDERRATED GEM

Shyam Benegal's *Nishant*, based on an original story by Vijay Tendulkar, is a quiet yet piercing scream against oppression, power and the tyranny of feudalism in rural India. Released as a follow-up to his exceptional debut *Ankur* (1974), this film further cemented Benegal's position as a film-maker who is skilled at laying bare the uncomfortable realities of Indian society. With a screenplay penned by Satyadev Dubey, the film's sharp and scathing dialogues accentuate its themes of injustice and resistance. *Nishant* may be set in 1945, but its narrative transcends time owing to its depiction of power structures, institutional corruption and the vulnerability of the oppressed.

Nishant is a tale of a village where an unchallenged feudal system is entirely under the thumb of a zamindar (played with terrifying authority by Amrish Puri) and his three equally ruthless brothers (portrayed by Mohan Agashe, Anant Nag and Naseeruddin Shah). Their control over the land and its people is so absolute that even law enforcement bows before them, rendering justice a meaningless concept. The brothers wield their power with impunity, treating women as objects to be taken at will and enforcing their rule through sheer terror.

One of the most chilling aspects of the film is the absolute normalization of oppression. The villagers live in constant fear and remain silent as a survival mechanism in a world where resistance seems futile. This atmosphere of submission makes the lone voice of defiance – Girish Karnad's schoolteacher – a beacon of hope, however fragile. His struggle against the feudal overlords is not just personal (after his wife, played by Shabana Azmi, is abducted by the zamindars), but symbolic of a broader resistance against darkness itself. The title, *Nishant* (meaning 'end of the night'), alludes to this desperate fight for justice and light in an era of moral and ethical darkness.

Benegal, working alongside cinematographer Govind Nihalani, crafts an aesthetic that appears to be drenched in realism. The film's visual language does not romanticize rural India; instead, it exposes its harshest realities. The dry, barren landscapes mirror the emotional and moral emptiness of the village, while Nihalani's use of long, static shots forces the viewer to confront the bleakness of the characters' fates. Unlike mainstream Bollywood films of the 1970s that often indulged in escapist storytelling, *Nishant* is unflinchingly brutal in its depiction of violence – not the kind that relies on spectacle, but the kind that exists in oppressive silence, in fear-ridden glances and in the quiet resignation to suffering. Vanraj Bhatia's minimalistic yet moving score contributes significantly to the film's miserable atmosphere by complementing its stark visuals efficiently. His music is not a mere background score but a narrative force that deepens the emotional gravity of the story.

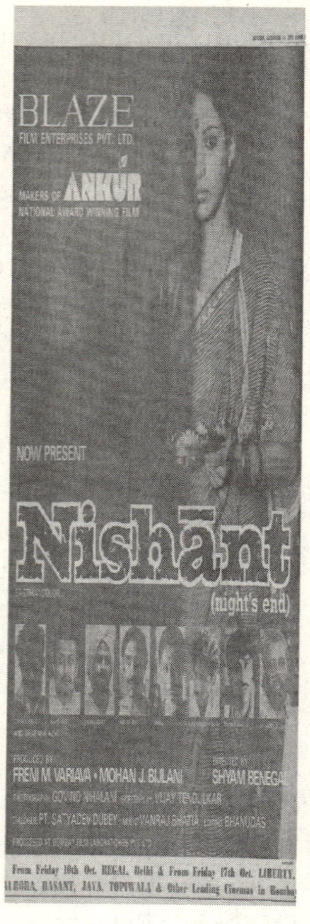

One of *Nishant*'s greatest strengths lies in its ensemble cast. Amrish Puri, often remembered for his larger-than-life villainous roles, delivers a chillingly understated performance as the oppressive feudal lord. His quiet menace, punctuated by moments of explosive cruelty, embodies the unchecked power that the film critiques. Naseeruddin Shah, in one of his early roles, brings a layered vulnerability to his character – a man complicit in the tyrannical system yet not entirely devoid of conscience. Mohan Agashe and Anant Nag complete the trio of terror with performances that are disturbingly realistic.

Girish Karnad is the moral centre of the film, portraying a schoolteacher who is idealistic but painfully aware of the odds stacked against him. His transition from a helpless victim to a reluctant revolutionary is one of the film's most compelling arcs. Shabana Azmi, as his abducted wife, conveys her character's trauma with remarkable skill – her silence speaks louder than any words could. Smita Patil, who plays a smaller but significant role, foreshadows the brilliance she would bring to Indian cinema in the years to come.

Perhaps the most disturbing aspect of *Nishant* is not just the brutality of the oppressors but the complicity of the system that enables them. The police, rather than being agents of justice, serve as mere extensions of the zamindar's will. The villagers, though sympathetic to the schoolteacher's plight, remain passive for most of the film, demonstrating how deeply fear has eroded their sense of agency.

The film does not entirely succumb to cynicism. The climax, where the teacher finally mobilizes the villagers against the tyrants, is a moment that is both cathartic and tragic. The uprising is not a glorified revolution; it is raw, chaotic and ultimately a desperate act of survival rather than a well-orchestrated rebellion. *Nishant* does not offer easy resolutions, because real life rarely does.

Fifty years after its release, *Nishant* remains eerily relevant. Feudal structures of the past may have ended, but power imbalances, systemic oppression and institutional corruption continue to define many aspects of India (and the world). The film's exploration of gender dynamics, the unchecked privilege of the ruling class and the crushing weight of silence in the face of injustice make it as impactful today as it was in 1975.

Unlike some of Benegal's later films like *Manthan* (1976) or *Kalyug* (1981), which had more structured socio-political narratives, *Nishant* operates on an almost primal level. It is not just about a particular era or a specific issue but about the very nature of power and resistance inherent to human beings. Perhaps this is why *Nishant*, despite being overshadowed by Benegal's other works, remains one of his most potent and unsettling films. Beyond its portrayal of feudalism in rural India, the film also deftly showcases the fear, silence and the long, arduous journey of the oppressed masses towards liberation. In that sense, *Nishant* is not merely a historical tale but an eternal one.

CAST: Girish Karnad, Naseeruddin Shah, Shabana Azmi, Smita Patil, Anant Nag, Mohan Agashe, Amrish Puri
OTHER CREDITS: Directed by Shyam Benegal. Music by Vanraj Bhatia.
RELEASE DATE: 18 March 1975
BOX OFFICE RESULT: Hit
RUNNING TIME: 2 Hours 23 Mins
TRIVIA: Naseeruddin Shah and Girish Karnad were at loggerheads during their time at the Film Institute. Karnad however was instrumental in Shah getting cast by Shyam Benegal for *Nishant*.

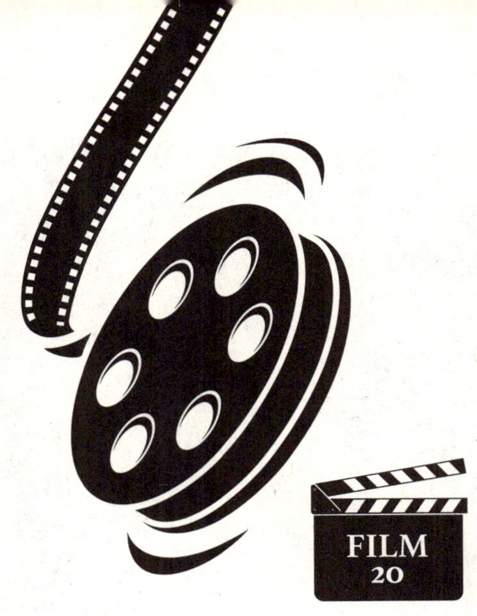

PRATIGGYA: DULAL GUHA'S MASALA POTBOILER AND ITS ENDURING LEGACY

Few films capture the essence of 1970s' Bo3llywood masala formula as effectively as *Pratiggya*. Directed by Dulal Guha, *Pratiggya* is a quintessential revenge drama featuring elements of action, comedy, romance and melodrama, which were hallmarks of mainstream Hindi cinema of the time. It was also a home production of its leading man, Dharmendra, who was then at the peak of his stardom, paired with Hema Malini, his most popular on-screen partner. The film's supporting cast included stalwarts like Ajit, Imtiaz Khan, Johnny Walker, Abhi Bhattacharya and Jagdeep, all of whom contributed to the film's larger-than-life storytelling.

Pratiggya followed the well-worn but always engaging revenge narrative. A truck driver, Ajit Singh (Dharmendra), impersonates

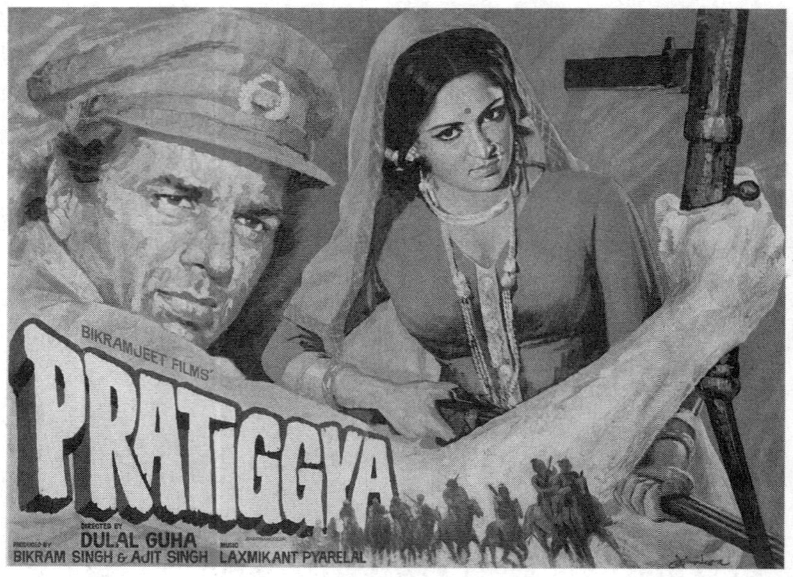

a police officer to bring order to a dacoit-ravaged village, only to discover that he is the long-lost son of an honest police officer murdered by the same dacoit. The film seamlessly transitions from a comic caper to an emotionally charged revenge drama, maintaining the high-energy scenes characteristic of 1970s' commercial cinema.

Dulal Guha, known for helming socially relevant dramas (*Dost*, *Dushman*, *Dharti Kahe Pukar Ke*), proves with *Pratiggya* his equal adeptness at crafting full-throttle entertainers. The film is a classic example of how masala cinema thrived on the amalgamation of various genres. Guha structures the film with a breezy, comedic first half in which Dharmendra's Ajit Singh revels in his disguise as a police officer, bringing his impeccable comic timing to the fore. His interactions with the villagers, especially his romantic sparring with Hema Malini's character, are also laced with humour. However, as the narrative progresses, the light-heartedness gives way to a revenge-fuelled climax with intense action sequences and melodramatic confrontations. Guha ensures that both these contrasting halves perfectly combine into a gripping story without dragging the film's pace.

The film's tonal shifts, such as comedy to romance to high drama, are executed with surprising finesse. The masala film formula often runs the risk of the film descending into chaos, but Guha's control over the material ensures that *Pratiggya* never loses its momentum. His direction, while not flashy, is efficient and energetic, emphasizing Dharmendra's megastar persona while allowing space for supporting characters to also shine.

Dharmendra's performance in *Pratiggya* stands out for being well-rounded. While his action-hero image was already well established, *Pratiggya* gave him a chance to display his comedic prowess. His flamboyant portrayal of the funny, brash and cocky but utterly charming Ajit Singh is commendable. The scenes where he effortlessly dupes the villagers into believing he is a real police officer were the highpoints of his comedic flair.

However, as the film progresses, the shift towards the more intense, revenge-driven arc allows Dharmendra to tap into his dramatic strengths. His transformation from a carefree truck driver to a man determined to avenge his father's death is convincing, and he also excels in the high-octane action sequences, proving once again why he was one of the most bankable action stars of the time.

Hema Malini, the reigning female superstar of the era, brings her characteristic charm and grace to *Pratiggya*. Her chemistry with Dharmendra is electric, and their playful romance provides some of the film's most enjoyable moments. Their flirtatious and witty banter adds much warmth to the narrative. Hema's role, though secondary to Dharmendra's, is not merely decorative; she plays a feisty and spirited character who holds her own in the male-dominated film.

A masala entertainer is incomplete without a memorable soundtrack, and *Pratiggya* delivers on that front with Laxmikant–Pyarelal's hit compositions. The most enduring song from the film, '*Main Jat Yamla Pagla Deewana*', became an anthem of sorts for Dharmendra, so much so that it inspired the title of the *Yamla Pagla Deewana* film series decades later. The song, with its infectious energy and rustic charm, perfectly encapsulates the carefree, mischievous side of Dharmendra's character. The rest of the soundtrack, including romantic melodies and situational numbers, efficiently complements the film's shifting moods.

Pratiggya was a box office hit, but its thunder was somewhat stolen by *Sholay*, which released around the same time. Given that *Sholay*, which also starred Dharmendra in one of the leading roles, redefined Hindi cinema with its grand scale, iconic characters and innovative storytelling, *Pratiggya* inevitably paled in comparison. However, despite this stiff competition, *Pratiggya* managed to carve out its own niche in Bollywood history as a quintessential 1970s' entertainer.

Nearly five decades later, *Pratiggya* continues to be an enjoyable watch, demonstrating the enduring appeal of the masala film template. It embodies the elements that defined the golden age of Bollywood's larger-than-life heroes, vibrant storytelling, catchy music and an emotional core that resonated with audiences. Dulal Guha may not have been as celebrated as some of his contemporaries, but with *Pratiggya*, he delivered a film that remains a prime example of commercially successful Hindi cinema.

For fans of 1970s' Bollywood, *Pratiggya* is a must-watch film that manages to entertain viewers with its humour, action and the undeniable star power of Dharmendra and Hema Malini.

CAST: Dharmendra, Hema Malini, Ajit, Johnny Walker, Jagdeep, Imtiaz Khan
OTHER CREDITS: Directed by Dulal Guha. Music by Laxmikant–Pyarelal.
RELEASE DATE: 23 June 1975
BOX OFFICE RESULT: Super Hit
RUNNING TIME: 2 Hours 20 Mins
TRIVIA: Dharmendra's brother Kanwar Ajit Singh, who produced the film, also played a small role as a truck driver in the film.

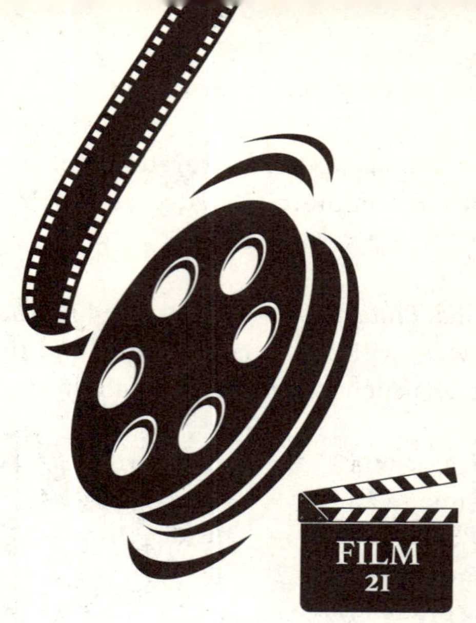

RAJ KHOSLA'S *PREM KAHANI*: A DRAMA FILM ABOUT LOVE, PATRIOTISM AND SACRIFICE

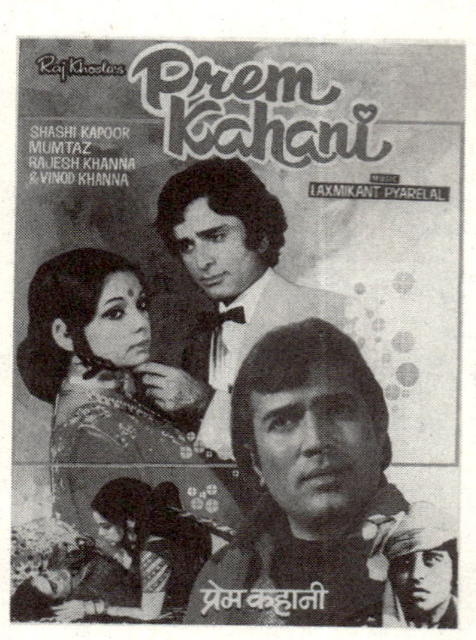

Raj Khosla's *Prem Kahani* is a bold film set against the backdrop of pre-independence India and revolves around the themes of love, sacrifice and duty portrayed in a heart-wrenching manner. At its heart is a love triangle involving the characters Rajesh (Rajesh Khanna), Kamini (Mumtaz) and Dheeraj (Shashi Kapoor), but the film also delves into the effects of patriotism and personal loss on an individual's journey. Rajesh, a poet indifferent to politics, is thrust into the freedom struggle after witnessing his older brother Brijesh (played by Trilok Kapoor) being brutally murdered by a British officer. His character shift from an apathetic romantic into a passionate revolutionary serves as the film's emotional turning point that triggers a series of events that profoundly affect those around him. The love he holds for Kamini is not only fractured by fate but also by his own choice to distance himself for the sake of her wellbeing, ultimately leading her to wed Dheeraj, a police officer tasked with capturing Rajesh, who is now a wanted fugitive. In a cruel twist of fate, as Rajesh flees from the authorities, he seeks shelter in the very home of Dheeraj, who finds himself torn between his role as a law enforcer and his loyalty to a friend. As complexities of betrayal, guilt and love unfold, the film moves towards a tragic climax – Kamini, caught between her past and present, makes the heartbreaking choice to shoot Rajesh, thereby proving her loyalty to her husband. However, his death is framed as a form of liberation, allowing him to finally escape the tangled web of love and war that ensnared him.

Despite its grand themes and engaging premise, *Prem Kahani* hints at a director in decline. Raj Khosla, who once directed classics like *Do Raaste* with aplomb, found himself struggling with creative stagnation, which was compounded by his battles with alcoholism. Although the film opened to a great deal of excitement, various delays and inconsistencies affected the final result, leading to scenes that occasionally come off as unintentionally funny. Chief among these is the incongruity of Rajesh Khanna's character, who is depicted as a poet from the pre-independence era dressed in terricot shirts with sweeping collars and nylon trousers – an inconsistency that makes it hard to take him seriously in a historical narrative. The dialogue often drifts into melodrama, and when viewed today, it can come across as cringe-inducing with its exaggerated performances and simplistic emotional arcs. However, despite these shortcomings, *Prem Kahani* manages to deliver a powerful emotional core, which ultimately serves as its only redeeming quality. The film's dramatic intensity is worth appreciation, particularly for its examination of relationships strained by duty and circumstance and in depicting a love that is at once fervent and fated.

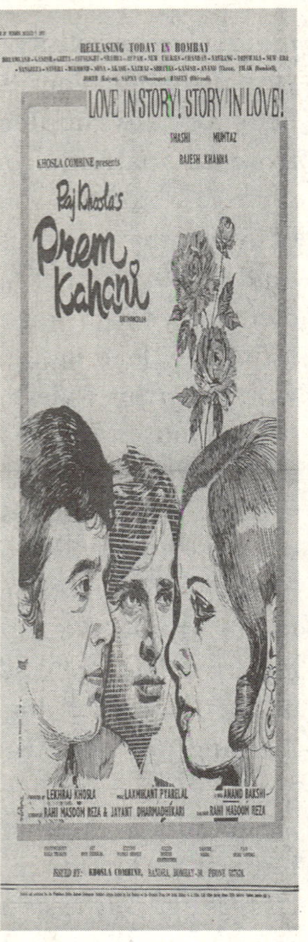

Interestingly, *Prem Kahani* shares thematic elements with another 1975 film – *Faraar* starring Amitabh Bachchan, Sharmila Tagore and Sanjeev Kumar – which also tells the story of a fugitive seeking refuge in the home of his ex-lover and her police officer spouse. However, what distinguishes *Prem Kahani* is its deeply emotional resonance. While *Faraar* leans more towards suspense, *Prem Kahani* is primarily driven by its characters' inner conflicts and emotional struggles. Kamini, despite embodying many of the clichés associated with Hindi film heroines of the era, is granted flashes of liberation that allow her to shine. Unlike the typical passive love interest, she refuses to dwell in despair when Rajesh distances himself, instead asserting her independence and refusing to plead for his acceptance.

Her choice to marry a man chosen by her father is an act of compliance but also a bold declaration that she will forge her own path. Later, during the film's climax, she again seizes control of her fate – and that of the two men ensnared in this impossible triangle – by making the shocking decision to shoot Rajesh, demonstrating her commitment to Dheeraj. Although this moment is melodramatic, it stands out as perhaps the film's most profound scene that illustrates the extent to which personal decisions can be influenced by duty, circumstance and survival.

Shashi Kapoor as Dheeraj portrays the conflicted husband with remarkable sincerity, capturing the anguish and torment of a man caught between his professional responsibilities and personal feelings. His character's journey is especially captivating as he comes to terms with the fact that his wife was once deeply in love with the very man he is ordered to apprehend. The inner conflict he experiences – his struggle to balance his sense of duty with the awareness of this history – is depicted with subtlety, making him one of the film's most well-rounded characters. Rajesh Khanna, despite the frequently questionable wardrobe choices and some overblown moments, delivers a compelling performance, especially in his transition from a carefree poet to a resolute revolutionary. His portrayal of Rajesh's internal anguish in the film's latter half adds soul to the character and renders his eventual demise all the more significant. Mumtaz, as Kamini, shines brightly by infusing her role with both strength and vulnerability, which ensures she isn't just a pawn caught between two men. Vinod Khanna, in a brief yet impactful role as a truck driver named Sher Khan, leaves a lasting impression when he sacrifices himself to safeguard Rajesh from the British.

One of *Prem Kahani's* significant strengths is its soundtrack composed by Laxmikant–Pyarelal. The film features several memorable songs, with the title track and '*Phool Aahista Phenko*' being favourites among Hindi music lovers even to this day.

Fifty years on, *Prem Kahani* might feel a bit out-of-touch in some areas, with certain moments causing unintended laughter rather than the intended emotional impact. The historical backdrop, while crucial to the storyline, often suffers from the film's visual anachronisms. Some of the dialogue appears to mismatch with the modern sensibilities that today's viewers might expect to see in films. Yet, despite these imperfections, the film's emotional and dramatic strengths are undeniable. Instead of the typical Hindi movies of the time, which mostly included grand heroes and action-driven plots, *Prem Kahani* chose to delve into human feelings and ethical conflicts.

CAST: Rajesh Khanna, Shashi Kapoor, Mumtaz, Murad, Yunus Parvez, K.N. Singh, Vinod Khanna
OTHER CREDITS: Directed by Raj Khosla. Music by Laxmikant–Pyarelal.
RELEASE DATE: 7 March 1975
BOX OFFICE RESULT: Average
RUNNING TIME: 2 Hours 28 Mins
TRIVIA: Despite his superstar status, Rajesh Khanna got third billing in the film, following Shashi Kapoor and Mumtaz.

Moushumi Chatterjee was the original choice for the heroine's role before being replaced by Mumtaz at the insistence of Rajesh Khanna.

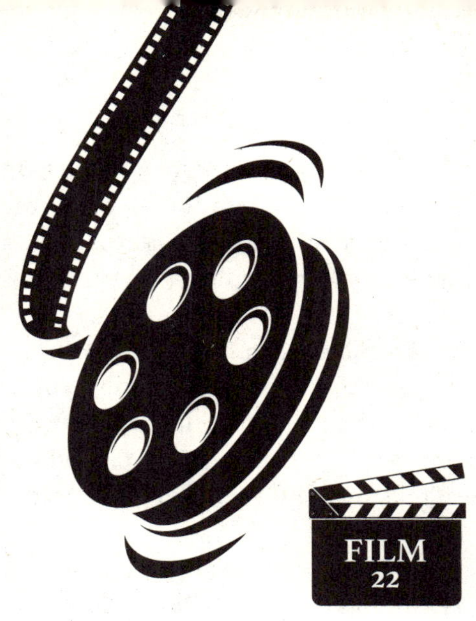

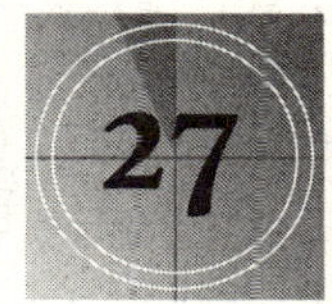

ATMA RAM'S *QAID*: RIVETING INTRIGUE RIDDLED WITH TROPES

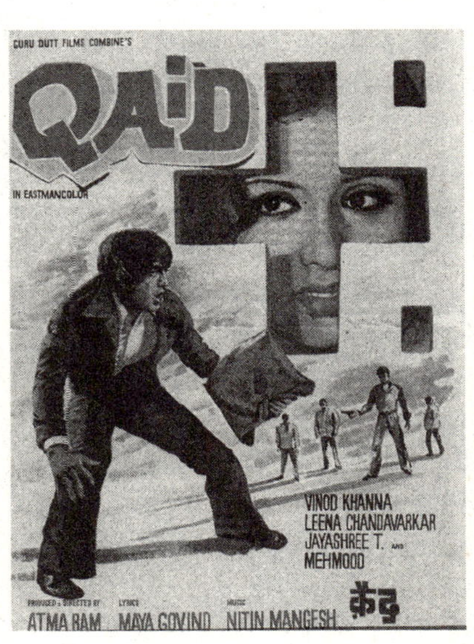

The 1970s were a fascinating era for Hindi cinema, with most movies characterized by a lively blend of action, romance, comedy and suspense presented in what became known as the 'masala' format. Atma Ram's *Qaid* (1975), following the success of his previous film *Memsaab* (1972), exemplifies this style. Starring Vinod Khanna, Leena Chandavarkar, Mehmood, Satyen Kappu and K.N. Singh,

Qaid took inspiration from the 1951 Hollywood noir *The Man with My Face*. However, Atma Ram's adaptation added a feminine twist to the narrative, resulting in a distinctly desi interpretation of the Hollywood doppelgänger mystery thriller.

Despite its intriguing concept and solid performances, *Qaid* unfortunately became somewhat overshadowed by other films from the same year. Although it utilized all the ingredients necessary for a commercially successful masala movie, it ultimately did not achieve an iconic status despite being a hit with film audiences.

The most captivating aspect of *Qaid* is its central mystery; a woman (Leena Chandavarkar) realizes she has been replaced by a lookalike who convinces everyone, even her closest family members, that she is the original. Stripped of her identity and desperate to validate her existence, she turns to advocate Jai (Vinod Khanna) for assistance in uncovering the truth. This premise, lifted from *The Man with My Face*, seemed to have the potential to be a gripping psychological thriller. However, in true Bollywood fashion, the film diminishes the suspense with unnecessary comedic subplots, song-and-dance sequences and action scenes.

While the masala style was essential for commercial success in mid-1970s' Hindi cinema, it arguably diverted focus from the core strength of *Qaid* – a doppelgänger mystery. The psychological tension that could have been developed through portraying a sense of urgency within a noir-like ambiance is frequently overtaken by comedic digressions, particularly those involving Mehmood. Although his performance earned him a Filmfare Award for Best Comedian, his character often feels more distracting than integral to the narrative.

The film also suffers from a hurried conclusion. While the first half effectively establishes the primary conflict, the second half devolves into predictable Bollywood dramatics, with legal battles, action sequences and a last-minute plot twist that ties everything up a tad too neatly. In contrast, *The Man with My Face* sustained a consistent tone of tension and despair, which *Qaid* largely sacrifices for desi commercial attractiveness.

Vinod Khanna, as the advocate Jai, brings his signature charm and commanding presence to the film. Khanna was on his way to becoming a leading star, and his acting chops in *Qaid* displayed his burgeoning potential as an action hero capable of showing emotional depth. Nevertheless, his character frequently oscillates between the serious lawyer and the romantic lead, at times undermining his credibility within the storyline.

Leena Chandavarkar, meanwhile, was offered a rare opportunity to show her talent off in a suspense thriller; however, the film failed to fully harness her abilities. Considering the plot's emphasis on her character's identity being usurped, viewers would expect a performance rich in emotion. Unfortunately, the screenplay seldom gives her a chance to confront the psychological turmoil of her character. Instead, the focus often shifts to Vinod Khanna's heroics or Mehmood's comedic moments. The rest of the cast, including K.N. Singh, Nazir Hussain, Satyen Kappu and Jayshree T, carry out their roles competently, although without leaving any significant impression.

Music Director duo Nitin–Mangesh composed the music for *Qaid*. While the soundtrack was quite popular at the time, it lacks an everlasting, enduring quality. The standout song is '*Yahan Kaun Hai Asli, Kaun Hai Nakli*', which cleverly conveys the film's themes of deception and mistaken identity. Its catchy tune and thoughtful lyrics resonated with listeners in the mid-1970s. Another notable piece, Kishore Kumar's '*Yeh Toh Zindagi Hai*', showcased his effortless vocal prowess. However, the rest of the soundtrack has largely faded from most people's memory.

Though *Qaid* did moderately well at the box office, it didn't leave a lasting legacy. Its most significant impact on Hindi cinema was perhaps influencing *Bol Radha Bol* (1992), starring Rishi Kapoor and Juhi Chawla. The latter film revived the doppelgänger theme but elevated it with a more polished script, improved pacing and higher production value. In contrast, *Qaid* feels like a film caught between its noir-thriller aspirations and the tropes of commercial Bollywood film-making. While its central idea had promise, the screenplay's inconsistent tone and the injection of superfluous elements held the movie back from success. Vinod Khanna delivered a steady performance true to his reputation.

Looking back, *Qaid* remains a fond memory for fans of mid-1970s' cinema; however, the film has not particularly aged well.

CAST: Vinod Khanna, Leena Chandavarkar, Mehmood, K.N. Singh, Nazir Hussain, Satyen Kappu, Jayshree T
OTHER CREDITS: Directed by Atma Ram. Music by Nitin–Mangesh.
RELEASE DATE: 21 May 1975
BOX OFFICE RESULT: Hit
RUNNING TIME: 2 Hours 10 Mins
TRIVIA: Nitin Mukesh collaborated with Kishore Kumar in the song '*Yeh Toh Zindagi Hai*' in this film.

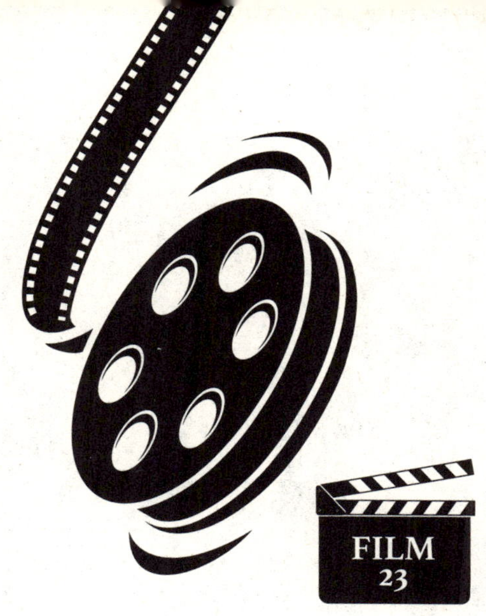

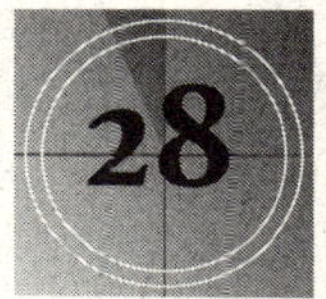

REVISITING *RAFOO CHAKKAR*: A CROSS-DRESSED COMEDY OF ERRORS

Cinema, across cultures, often thrives on adaptations – retelling old stories in new ways by infusing them with local flavour and the emotional vocabulary of the target audience. *Rafoo Chakkar*, directed by Narender Bedi and starring Rishi Kapoor and Neetu Singh, exemplifies this spirit of cinematic appropriation. While its basic theme traces back to Billy Wilder's *Some Like It Hot* (1959), which itself was adapted from the French film *Fanfare of Love* (1935), *Rafoo Chakkar* emerges as an independently enjoyable classic Bollywood masala entertainer with its own cultural resonance.

At the heart of *Rafoo Chakkar* is the age-old trope of mistaken and concealed identities, a comic device that has been played to death spanning centuries, from Shakespearean theatre to

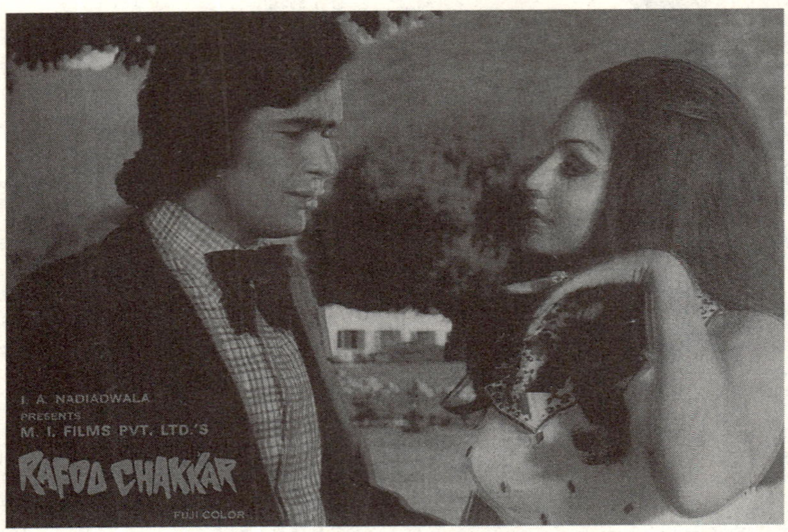

20th-century cinema. The plot revolves around two struggling musicians, Dev (Rishi Kapoor) and Salim (Paintal), who, after witnessing a murder, disguise themselves as women to hide in an all-female music troupe. Much of the film's humour derives from this gender masquerade, pushing the boundaries of drag in performance while also inviting the audience into a world where appearance is both a shield and a source of confusion.

Rishi Kapoor's natural charisma and soft facial features are leveraged effectively to portray a convincing and endearing female persona, earning him the label of a 'cute girl' in jest and admiration. Yet the film's engagement with gender roles is not driven by subversion but by necessity and comedic effect. In contrast to contemporary discourses on gender fluidity or queer identity, *Rafoo Chakkar* treats cross-dressing as a temporary plot mechanism that generates laughs without deeply examining the structures it plays with.

What emerges is a playful engagement with gender as costume rather than identity. This lens, however, invites retrospective criticism in today's more conscious and nuanced cultural climate. What was once perceived as harmless fun may now feel reductive or politically tone-deaf. Nevertheless, when contextualized within the socio-cultural framework of 1970s' India, the film's treatment of these themes reflects a more innocent, even naive, brand of comedy that lacked both malice and awareness.

One of the triumphs of *Rafoo Chakkar* lies in its seamless Indianization of a foreign script. Wilder's sharp, fast-talking, sexually suggestive comedy is transformed into a more emotionally palatable Indian narrative. The flirtation becomes romantic yearning, sexual tension is replaced by coy glances and misunderstandings, and the criminal underworld gains a slapstick tint. Most notably, Bollywood's signature ingredient, music, is infused masterfully into the narrative by the celebrated composer duo Kalyanji–Anandji.

Kalyanji–Anandji's peppy music boosted the film's popularity, especially songs like '*Tumko Mere Dil Ne*', '*Kisi Pe Dil Agar Aa Jaaye*' and '*Chhuk Chhuk Chhak Chhak*', offering a melodious counterpoint to the chaos and comedy of the primary plot.

Moreover, the added subplot of Rishi Kapoor's character pretending to be the son of a wealthy tycoon to woo Neetu Singh infuses a distinctly Bollywood-esque essence of aspirational romance and family sentiment as well as dramatic tension and emotional payoff.

One of the more contentious aspects of *Rafoo Chakkar*, especially when viewed through a contemporary lens, is its brand of humour, which does at times border on crass or politically incorrect. Jokes rooted in gender stereotypes, physical appearance and mistaken identity may come off as insensitive today. However, such comedic choices must be assessed within their temporal and cultural context. In the 1970s, Indian cinema – and indeed, society at large – was not engaged in the kinds of discourse around identity politics, gender performativity or inclusivity that have gained prominence in recent decades.

This is not to excuse the problematic elements, but to understand them as products of their time shaped by prevailing sensibilities and cinematic conventions. If anything, they reveal how comedy evolves alongside cultural values and how films like *Rafoo Chakkar* serve as markers of the social imagination of their era.

Despite its derivativeness, *Rafoo Chakkar* is not merely a copy of its Hollywood predecessor. It holds its own as a charming, zany and musically rich comedy that mirrors an era where storytelling was simple, performances exuberant and music memorable. The film's enduring appeal rests on the chemistry of its leads alongside the novelty of its premise and its commitment to entertainment above all else.

In a time of globalized content and complex narratives, *Rafoo Chakkar* may appear quaint. Yet therein lies its appeal; it is a cinematic time capsule representative of a version of Bollywood that was less burdened by realism or political correctness, and more attuned to spectacle, sentiment and spontaneity.

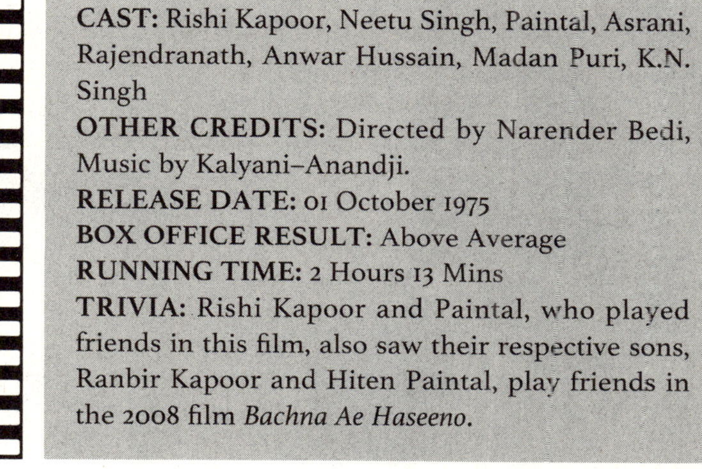

CAST: Rishi Kapoor, Neetu Singh, Paintal, Asrani, Rajendranath, Anwar Hussain, Madan Puri, K.N. Singh
OTHER CREDITS: Directed by Narender Bedi, Music by Kalyani–Anandji.
RELEASE DATE: 01 October 1975
BOX OFFICE RESULT: Above Average
RUNNING TIME: 2 Hours 13 Mins
TRIVIA: Rishi Kapoor and Paintal, who played friends in this film, also saw their respective sons, Ranbir Kapoor and Hiten Paintal, play friends in the 2008 film *Bachna Ae Haseeno*.

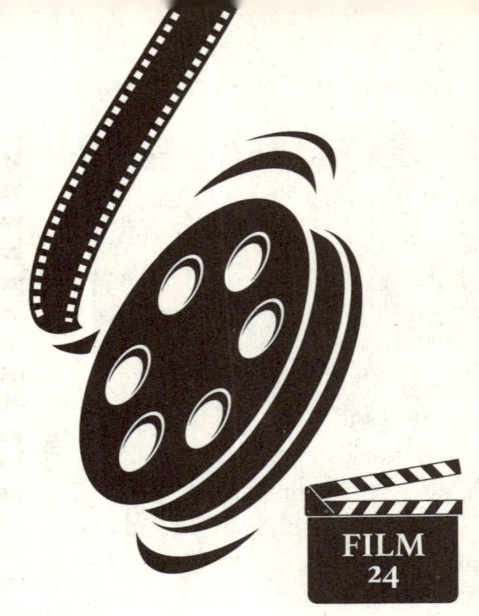

DINESH RAMESH'S *RAFTAAR*: AN UNPRETENTIOUS ENTERTAINER

Dinesh Ramesh's *Raftaar* occupies an interesting niche in mainstream Hindi cinema. Released in a year brimming with multiple Bollywood blockbusters, it emerged as a surprise hit, perhaps less for the novelty it offered and more for the way it successfully leaned into the 1970s' masala cinema. Featuring a mix of action, romance, melodrama, social commentary and music, *Raftaar* is emblematic of the kind of cinema that dominated Indian screens in the post-Golden-Age period – films that did not shy away from sensationalism or exaggerated emotional arcs.

Raftaar tells the story of love, betrayal and vengeance pivoting around a rural-urban dichotomy embodied in Moushumi Chatterjee's dual roles (dual pretend-characters in a single role, actually). The plot is packed with twists and dramatic shifts from romance to rape, suicide to rebirth and eventually to justice. The narrative progression bears the unmistakable rhythm of commercial Hindi cinema, which often operated in cycles of trauma and redemption. The trope of a wronged woman returning in a new avatar to seek justice is a recurrent theme in Bollywood, but *Raftaar* manages to give it a slightly more visceral edge through the character arcs of Rani/Rita.

What is most striking, and perhaps most unconventional for its time, is the way the film centres its emotional and narrative weight around the female protagonist. Though often spoken of as an early solo hit for Vinod Mehra, it is Moushumi Chatterjee's portrayal that acts as the emotional anchor of the film. Her transformation from an innocent village belle to a sharp urban woman on the path of avenging her assault is handled with a sense of conviction that elevates the otherwise formulaic storytelling. The duality of her character – first Rani, then Rita – also subtly critiques the limitations and biases that society places on women based on their appearance and demeanour.

The film does not shy away from portraying the brutal realities faced by its female characters. The rape of Rani by Kumar Sahab is a disturbing but critical moment that serves as a catalyst for the film's second act. While the representation is melodramatic, it reflects a major trend in 1970s' Hindi films where violence against women was troublingly either a plot device or a method of character development, many a times for the male lead. What is commendable, however, is how *Raftaar* allows its female lead not only to survive but to reclaim her life, which was a rarity in that decade.

The villainous Kumar Sahab, played by Danny Denzongpa,

embodies the archetype of the lascivious, power-drunk antagonist. His propensity to manipulate both men and women mirrors the decaying moral order that many 1970s' films aimed to critique. Vikram's eventual confrontation with Kumar and his past actions is predictable but satisfying by staying true to the film's moral equilibrium.

Although Vinod Mehra as Vikram is affable and earnest, he lacks the magnetism typically expected of a solo male lead. His performance, though competent, is overshadowed by the brilliance of Moushumi Chatterjee, who delivers a highly emotive performance. Her ability to switch between the rustic charm of Rani and the urbane poise of Rita demonstrates her versatility and gives the film much of its emotional and dramatic boost.

Danny, always reliable in negative roles, delivers a menacing performance as Kumar. His presence adds a sense of edgy danger that the film benefits from. His change of heart to be a 'good person' is a tad inexplicable, but it suits the narrative flow of the film.

Ranjeet and Janki Das contribute adequately in their respective roles, but it is the supporting character of Jackson, played splendidly by Madan Puri in a glorious change of image, who adds unexpected depth. As a kind-hearted musician who saves Rani from death and raises her as his own, Jackson becomes a symbol of compassion and redemption, an antithesis to the moral corruption of Kumar.

The film also gives actress Arpana Choudhary an opportunity to extend beyond her typecast roles as a side dancer. Her performance is credible and realistic, suggesting a slow but noticeable shift in how Bollywood was beginning to treat its secondary female characters.

Sonik–Omi's soundtrack is integral to the film's popularity and longevity. Songs like '*Sansar Hai Ek Nadiya*' and '*Main Teri Heer*' are melodious and emotionally resonant, effectively capturing the film's romantic and tragic beats.

Raftaar doesn't pretend to be anything it is not. It is unapologetically commercial, deeply melodramatic and reliant on well-worn clichés. Nonetheless, it works as an entertaining movie, perhaps because of this very honesty. The film delivers exactly what its audience expects – drama, justice, love, loss and redemption – while also succeeding for its awareness of the emotional logic of its viewers.

The film's resonance lies not in novelty but in familiarity. In a rapidly modernizing India of the mid-1970s, when social and political tensions were running high, films like *Raftaar* offered emotional catharsis through familiar stories with morally satisfying conclusions. It's this predictability wrapped in high-stakes emotion and music that made it memorable.

Raftaar is a film that perfectly understood the DNA of commercial Hindi cinema. However, it is not without its flaws – the melodrama can seem too excessive, the plot occasionally implausible and the treatment of gender violence problematic by modern standards. But within the ecosystem of 1970s' Bollywood, it is a film that catered effectively to its audience and their emotional needs. It gave Moushumi Chatterjee one of her most impactful roles, nudged Vinod Mehra towards solo stardom and also provided a platform for side actors like Arpana

Choudhary to shine. In its unpretentiousness lies its charm, and in its formula lies its success.

CAST: Vinod Mehra, Moushumi Chatterjee, Danny, Ranjeet, Madan Puri, Janki Das, Arpana Choudhary
OTHER CREDITS: Directed by Dinesh–Ramanesh. Music by Sonik–Omi.
RELEASE DATE: 13 March 1975
BOX OFFICE RESULT: Hit
RUNNING TIME: 2 Hours 10 Mins
TRIVIA: This was the first film that cast Moushumi Chatterjee with Vinod Mehra for the year 1975. They went on to star together in two more films that year; namely, *Do Jhoot* and *Mazaaq*. Earlier in 1974, they had starred together for the first time in *Us Paar*, and they paired up the following year in 1976 in *Sabse Bada Rupaiya* and *Zindagi*. Moushumi would go on to do many more films with Vinod Mehra in the lead, making him her most frequent leading man.

Dinesh–Ramanesh would be perhaps one of the earliest director duos in Bollywood. Ramanesh Puri was the son of veteran actor Madan Puri. Dinesh Lakhanpal and Ramanesh Puri were assistants to Shakti Samanta before they started directing films independently.

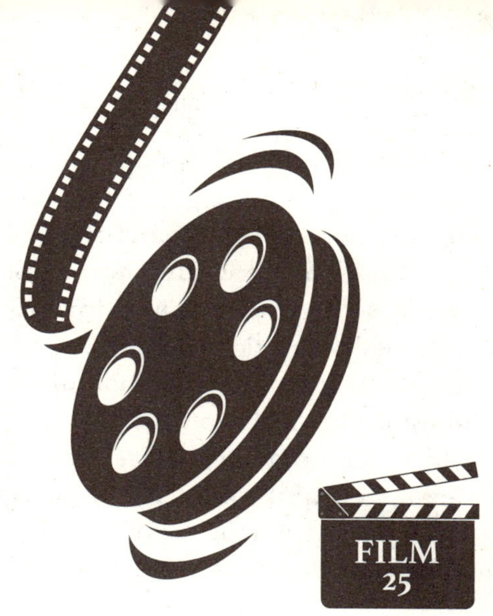

SOHANLAL KANWAR'S *SANYASI*: OF KITSCHY IDEALS AND MASALA-LACED MORALS

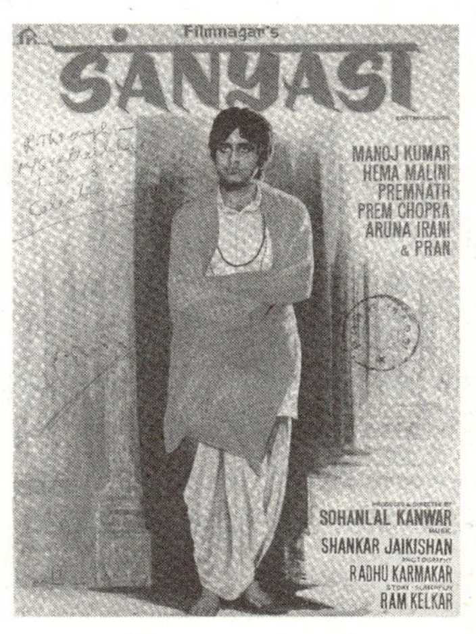

Sanyasi was a major box office success and an important film from Bollywood's golden era of masala movies. Directed by Sohanlal Kanwar, it was rumoured that Manoj Kumar had a significant influence on the film behind the scenes. Featuring a stellar cast including Manoj Kumar, Hema Malini, Pran, Prem Chopra, Premnath, Raj Mehra, Sulochana and Aruna Irani, the film featured a mix of drama, romance, betrayal and morality, keeping

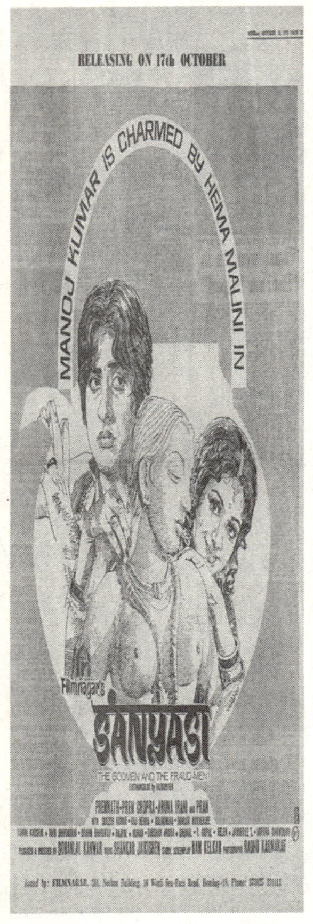

audiences entertained throughout.

Sanyasi was a straightforward mainstream movie, crafted purely for entertainment rather than for any intellectual or artistic aspirations, which was key to its resounding box office triumph. The film captivated viewers with its screenplay characterized by unexpected twists and rich drama, resulting in its status as one of the year's top-five hits.

The plot of Sanyasi centred around Ram, played by Manoj Kumar, who was raised with strong beliefs in celibacy and devotion to God, heavily influenced by his mother and paternal grandfather's wishes that he not mirror his father's reckless and overindulgent ways. This steadfast belief led Ram to shun worldly pleasures, including fleeing from his own wedding, which astonishes his family. This unexpected rejection of marriage sparks a series of events, especially concerning his grandfather, who, before to his death, drafts a will with specific stipulations. According to the will, Ram is required to marry within a year to claim the family inheritance. Additionally, his mother is instructed by the will to pass the property to a relative to prevent it from being donated to charity. These legal stipulations form the crux of the film's main conflict, creating a fertile ground for deception and manipulation.

Complicating matters further was the family Pandit, Shanti Baba (played by Pran), who comforted Ram's mother, asserting that marriage would occur if it was meant to be and counselled against pressuring Ram. However, fate intervened when her brother and nephew, depicted by Raj Mehra and Prem Chopra, unexpectedly show up at her home. Seeing an opportunity to seize the property for themselves, they concoct a scheme to introduce a fake woman, Aarti (Hema Malini), into the household, posing as a genuine friend. This manipulation intensifies with the arrival of a fraudulent holy man, played by Premnath, who further increases the deception and chaos in the unfolding drama. These plot points create a story steeped in betrayal, pretence and the eventual triumph of good over evil. The narrative follows Ram, a man deeply committed to a spiritual life, as he manoeuvres through the tangled web of deception surrounding him, ultimately safeguarding his mother and his rightful inheritance.

Sanyasi was not crafted as a film of artistic depth, and its massive success can be attributed to its well-structured screenplay that kept audiences engaged with its constant surprises. The film's writing ensured that the drama unfolded compellingly. The viewers of the 1970s were drawn to stories that provided wholesome entertainment, and *Sanyasi* delivered on that promise. It was a film that resonated with the masses, combining moral dilemmas, family conflicts, clever deception and the promise of eventual justice. The film also shone due to its strong performances, particularly from Manoj Kumar, who was already celebrated for his patriotic and socially relevant roles. His portrayal of Ram, a man caught between his upbringing and life's harsh realities, struck a chord with audiences. Hema Malini, with her signature grace and charm, further enriched the film's allure.

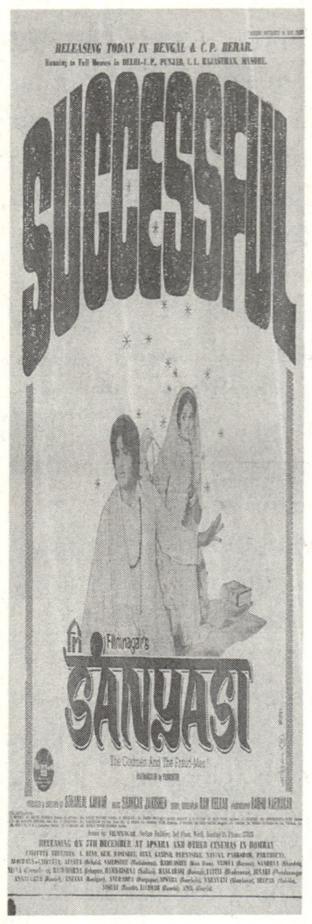

Another highlight of *Sanyasi* was its music composed by Shankar of the iconic Shankar–Jaikishan duo. Despite Jaikishan's passing, Shankar continued to evoke their musical style, keeping their legacy continued. The song '*Chal Sanyasi Mandir Mein*' became an iconic track that was closely associated with the film and mirrored its central theme of renunciation and spirituality. The film's music was crucial in enhancing its appeal since Bollywood productions of that era heavily relied on their soundtracks to attract audiences.

The year 1975 was a monumental chapter for Bollywood, showcasing numerous major films that achieved remarkable box office success. Over twenty-five films celebrated various anniversaries, including silver, golden and platinum, indicating the extraordinary cinematic achievements of that year. The fact that *Sanyasi* managed to distinguish itself among such a wealth of hits, despite its straightforward commercial nature, is proof of its broad appeal. While the film may not have showcased any groundbreaking cinematic brilliance, it resonated with viewers who watched Hindi cinema for movies with entertainment, drama and moral resolution. Although the film's qualitative aspects might not have been its strongest points, its ability to keep audiences immersed ensured its place among the year's top five hits.

Sanyasi serves as a quintessential example of how Bollywood in the 1970s catered to its audience with well-tailored commercial cinema while also providing entertainment with themes of morality, deception and righteousness. Its success was driven by a compelling story, strong performances, a harmonious soundtrack and an engaging screenplay. Even though it didn't aim for lofty intellectual goals, it remains a cherished memory in the annals of Bollywood cinema.

CAST: Manoj Kumar, Hema Malini. Pran, Prem Chopra, Premnath, Sulochana, Raj Mehra, Aruna Irani
OTHER CREDITS: Directed by Sohanlal Kanwar. Music by Shankar–Jaikishen.
RELEASE DATE: 17 October 1975
BOX OFFICE RESULT: Super Hit
RUNNING TIME: 2 Hours 40 Mins
TRIVIA: There were as many as six lyricists writing songs for the film, which is probably the only time it happened in a Hindi film. The lyricists were Indivar, Verma Malik, Vithalbhai Patel, Visheshwar Sharma, M.G. Hashmat and Hasrat Jaipuri.

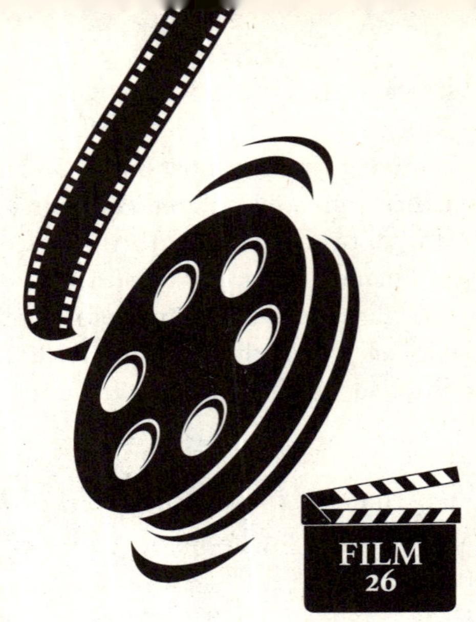

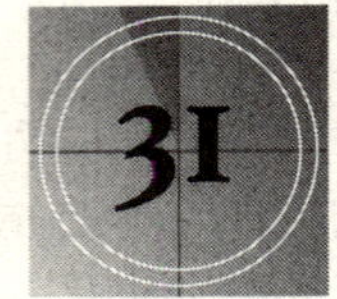

RAMESH SIPPY'S *SHOLAY*: INDIA'S CULTURAL LANDMARK

Few films can genuinely be considered more than just cinema but a gigantic cultural phenomenon that becomes an integral part of a nation's very identity. *Sholay* is one such film – not only a box-office triumph but also a cultural landmark and cinematic moment that forever altered Indian film-making and storytelling. As film-maker Shekhar Kapur aptly summarized, Bollywood can be categorized simply as 'Before *Sholay*' and 'After *Sholay*'. As it marks its fifty-year milestone, *Sholay* stands as an experience of its own with the ability to mesmerize audiences, and its legacy continues to influence film-makers. In it, every scene, every line of dialogue and every character, no matter how small, has woven itself into the shared consciousness of an entire nation.

But what makes *Sholay* so significant? Why does a film that

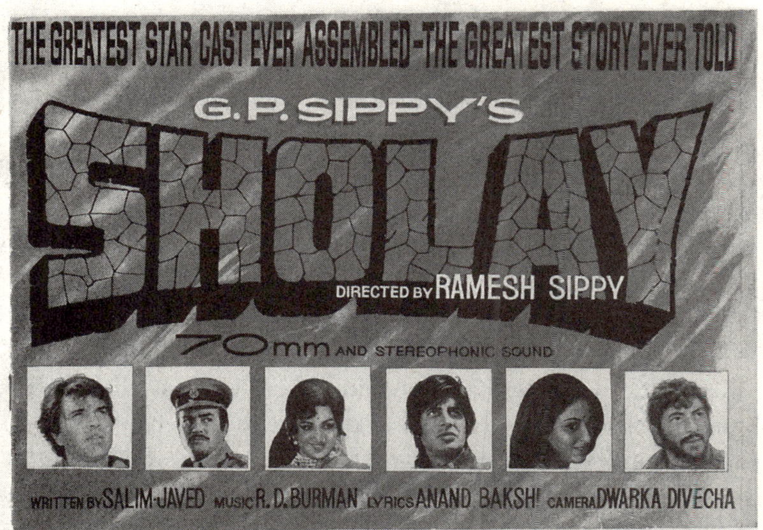

drew from various influences still resonate so powerfully? The answer lies not just in its narrative but in its execution – wherein everything from direction to performances, cinematography to music and action to emotions converges in a rare and perfect film.

Sholay is essentially a story about friendship, revenge and heroic feats, but it is also so much more. It delves into duty, loss, sacrifice and a dramatic exploration of good and evil that challenges the simplistic divisions often seen in mainstream films. The celebrated screenwriting duo, Salim–Javed, didn't invent a completely new story. The film openly shares its influences, drawing from Hollywood westerns like *The Magnificent Seven* and *Once Upon a Time in the West*, alongside Kurosawa's *Seven Samurai*. Closer to home, films like *Mera Gaon Mera Desh* and *Khote Sikkay* had already explored similar themes. However, *Sholay* never feels like a mere copy of any of these. Instead, it refines and transforms these influences into something distinctly Indian, merging the scale of a spaghetti western with the prominent emotionality of Indian storytelling. It doesn't just borrow ideas; it reimagines them, placing them into a setting that is unquestionably its own.

One of the film's standout achievements is Ramesh Sippy's masterful direction. The rugged landscapes of Ramgarh, beautifully captured by Dwarka Divecha, create an almost legendary backdrop. The expansive emptiness reflects the moral dilemmas faced by its characters, while the wide shots and carefully arranged action scenes elevate the visual storytelling. Unlike the often stilted or exaggerated action of earlier Indian films, *Sholay* introduced a level of realism and intensity that was groundbreaking and unprecedented. The tense, dynamic and visually stunning train robbery sequence at the film's start is a masterclass in action. Even the quieter scenes, such as Radha extinguishing a lamp in her silent melancholic sorrow, are crafted with such poetic grace that they linger well beyond the end credits.

The performances in *Sholay* are simply iconic. Dharmendra and Amitabh Bachchan's portrayals of Veeru and Jai, respectively, epitomize the portrayal of friendship in Indian cinema. Their playful camaraderie and steadfast loyalty to each other form the emotional backbone of the film. Veeru, the charming, boisterous and impulsive one, stands in stark contrast to Jai, the introspective, quiet and self-sacrificing hero. The brilliance of their relationship lies in how seamlessly it shifts between humour and heartache, making their bond feel authentic and emotionally impactful. Sanjeev Kumar's Thakur Baldev Singh, a man driven by vengeance, adds a dramatic depth to the narrative. His pain is not loud; it simmers and stays contained. His confrontation with Gabbar Singh – where his inability to wield a weapon symbolizes both his vulnerability and enduring strength – is among the most memorable moments in the film and significantly elevates the climax, resulting in a simultaneously satisfactory and melancholic payoff.

Hema Malini's Basanti, characterized by her endless chatter and vibrant energy, represents a rare female character in Indian action cinema who is more than just a romantic interest but also vital to the plot. Jaya Bhaduri's Radha, despite limited dialogue, expresses a wealth of emotion through her silence and demeanour, showcasing a stoic strength alongside deep sorrow that beautifully contrasts with the film's otherwise explosive narrative. Even the film's smallest characters – Soorma Bhopali, the Jailer and Imaam Saab – leave an indelible mark on the intricately layered screenplay.

Yet, if one character embodies *Sholay* more than others, it is Gabbar Singh. Brought to life with a tantalizing mix of menace and flair by Amjad Khan, Gabbar Singh is much more than a villain; he is a monument to pure evil. Indian cinema had seen its fair share of antagonists before, but none instilled the same sheer psychological dread as Gabbar. His voice, his laughter, his sadistic delight in cruelty – each trait made him the gold standard for future villains in Indian cinema. Lines like '*Kitne aadmi thhe?*' and '*Tera kya hoga, Kaalia?*' became so ingrained in popular culture that they transcended the film itself. Gabbar Singh was not a terrifying sociopath due to a tragic backstory that attempts to justify or explain his actions; he was simply evil for evil's sake. He embodied chaos and a destructive force devoid of any redeeming traits, making him all the more unforgettable. *Sholay* is not solely about heroic actions and villainy; it is also quite rich in emotional depth. The film boldly addresses heartbreak and loss. Jai's death, one of the most heart-wrenching moments in the film, is portrayed with such restraint that it leaves a greater impact than a melodramatic farewell ever could. Thakur's quest for vengeance, when it finally unfolds, brings about not triumph but catharsis. Veeru's heartbroken response to Jai's sacrifice is not just a sad scene but a moment that encapsulates friendship and grief so well that most viewers are left in tears. The film doesn't present easy resolutions; it allows its emotions to settle, ensuring its impact stays with the audience long after the final scene.

Technically the film is considered brilliant in every department. From Divecha's magnificent cinematography to M.S. Shinde's slick editing, the superbly executed action sequences and R.D. Burman's pulsating music and atmospheric background score, *Sholay* makes optimal use of its awesome bundle of talented technicians. The entire mood and feel of the film are enhanced by the flawless work of brilliant musical artists.

Perhaps the greatest testament to *Sholay*'s enduring legacy is its timeless nature. Even fifty years on, it is not simply watched but also quoted, referenced and celebrated in countless ways. Every scene, every line and every character have woven themselves into the cultural fabric of India. Unlike many classics that remain trapped in nostalgia, *Sholay* feels like as vibrant a viewing experience today as it did in 1975. It is a film that doesn't grow old but only gains stature, proving that true cinematic brilliance lies not in following trends but in excellent storytelling that delivers almost once-in-a-generation cinematic briliance.

CAST: Dharmendra, Sanjeev Kumar, Hema Malini, Amitabh Bachchan, Jaya Bhaduri, Amjad Khan
OTHER CREDITS: Directed by Ramesh Sippy. Story by Salim–Javed. Music by R.D. Burman.
RELEASE DATE: 15 August 1975
BOX OFFICE RESULT: All-Time Blockbuster
RUNNING TIME: 3 Hours 23 Mins
TRIVIA: Danny and Shatrughan Sinha were part of the original proposed cast. Danny couldn't do the role as he had committed his dates to Feroz Khan's *Dharmatma*, which was being shot in Afghanistan. Shatrughan was replaced by Amitabh Bachchan after Bachchan put in a word to co-actor Dharmendra.

Several scenes were removed from the film because of excessive length. A scene at a dhaba where Jai and Veeru eat, just preceding the song '*Yeh Dosti*', was cut, as was a qawwali, '*Chaand Sa Koi Chehra*', which was shot in the jail.

The original cut of the film had Thakur killing Gabbar. The Emergency-period censors however objected to showing an ex-lawman taking the law in his own hands, and hence the end was changed to Gabbar being taken away by the police. The original end of the film however is still available on some DVDs.

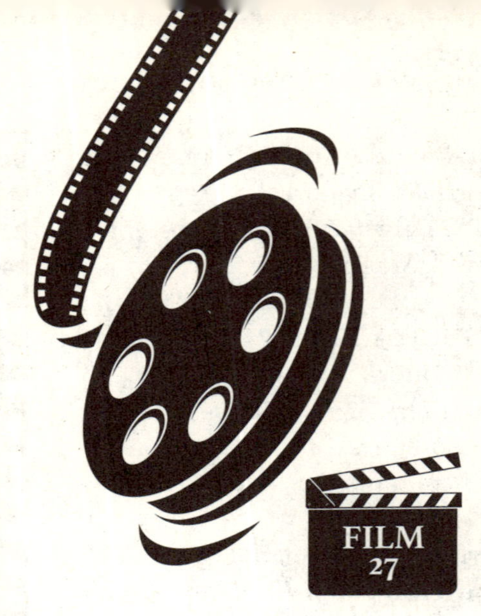

RAGHUNATH JHALANI'S *ULJHAN*: A SUSPENSEFUL FAMILY DRAMA

Raghunath Jhalani's *Uljhan* (1975) is a riveting example of how mainstream Bollywood in the mid-1970s cleverly mixed suspense, family dynamics and social themes into engaging tales that connected with audiences. While the film has a convincing plot that could have easily turned into a tense legal thriller, Jhalani opted for a focus on emotional struggles and melodrama – a feature of his distinctive narrative style. The film is particularly noteworthy for being the acting debut of Sulakshana Pandit, who was also a playback singer, paired with the dependable

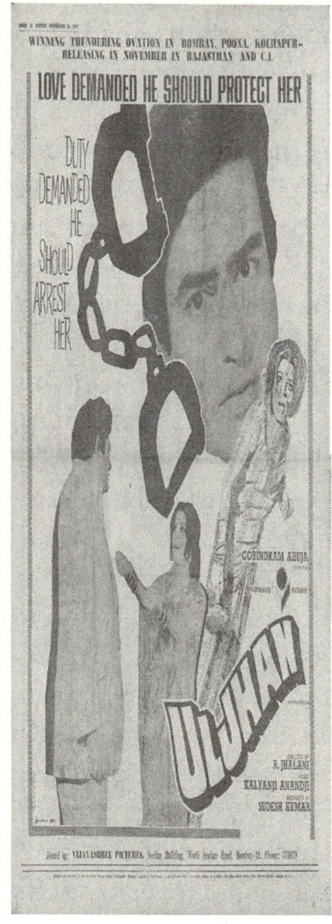

Sanjeev Kumar. The impressive cast also featured luminaries like Ashok Kumar, Ranjeet, Aruna Irani, Asrani and Farida Jalal, all of whom contributed majorly to *Uljhan*'s box office success. Even though it's a remake of *Kangan* (1959), the film managed to stand out during a time when remakes were prevalent, especially when the original stories had already entertained audiences.

Despite not being a name that casual moviegoers would easily recall, Jhalani was a director behind several successful films of his time. His body of work included the romantic hit *Aaye Din Bahaar Ke* (1966), the melodrama *Aaya Saawan Jhoom Ke* (1969), the suspenseful thriller *Anamika* (1973) and the family drama *Badaltey Rishtey* (1978). Each of these films featured his hallmark style of combining relatable narratives with emotional intensity and catchy music. His directorial approach heavily featured dramatic elements that were known to resonate with viewers, and *Uljhan* was no different. While its premise suggested a crime thriller film, what unfolded was more of a social, family drama dressed up as a murder mystery.

The plot of *Uljhan* centres around Karuna, portrayed by Sulakshana Pandit, who finds herself caught in a criminal web on her wedding day. After a tense encounter with the shady Brij Bhushan (Ranjeet), she accidentally causes his death in self-defence. The real twist comes when her new husband, Anand (Sanjeev Kumar), is assigned to investigate the case, unknowingly delving into the very crime she was part of. The ensuing narrative is filled with high tension as Karuna tries to hide the truth while Anand inches closer to discovering it. This struggle between marital loyalty and moral conflict becomes the film's emotional heart. Ashok Kumar's portrayal as Judge Kailash Chand adds weight to the storyline, particularly when he steps in to defend his daughter-in-law once the truth surfaces. The courtroom scenes, while perhaps lacking in sharpness, provide an opportunity for a significant revelation by Aruna Irani's character Usha, whose testimony unravels the story's concluding mysteries.

One of the most remarkable elements of *Uljhan* is its decision to steer away from the darker tones often associated with thrillers and murder mysteries. Instead, it weaves in themes of romance, family devotion and emotional struggle, aligning it perfectly with the 1970s' popular Hindi films. Although this might have lessened the film's chances of being a riveting thriller, it made it far more approachable for mainstream viewers of the time. The narrative doesn't lean on procedural police investigations or gritty realism; it thrives instead on dramatic irony and the emotional baggage of its main characters. The tension derives not from a complex unravelling of clues but from the psychological strain experienced between husband and wife. Sanjeev Kumar, renowned for imbibing his roles with depth, plays Anand with a blend of earnestness and resolve, while Sulakshana Pandit, in her debut performance, holds her own, although her talents shone brighter in the realm of music than acting.

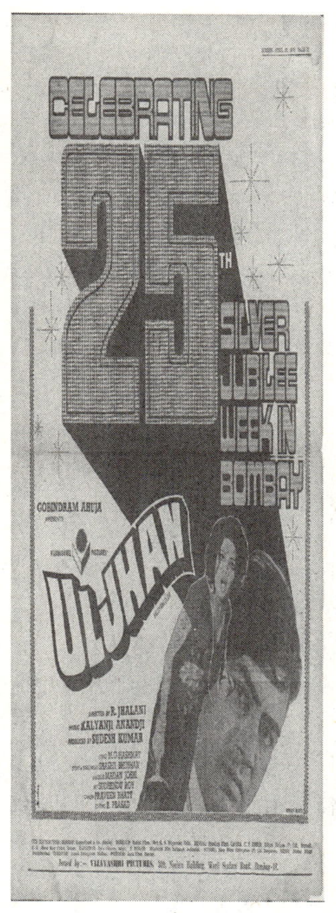

As for the music, *Uljhan* benefits immensely from its soundtrack crafted by Kalyanji–Anandji. The title song, sung twice separately by Kishore Kumar and Lata Mangeshkar, became a well-loved hit. Another popular track, '*Subah Aur Shaam Kaam Hi Kaam*', received considerable airplay. In true 1970s' Bollywood fashion, the music played a vital role in amplifying the film's emotional resonance, ensuring that even if the plot faded from memory, its songs stayed alive in public consciousness.

While *Uljhan* may not hold a prominent place in current discussions about Hindi cinema classics, it is a quintessential example of the films that thrived at the box office during the mid-1970s, especially films that seemlessly blended suspense, drama and social commentary into entertaining narratives. It also illustrates Raghunath Jhalani's prowess in creating films that, while not cutting-edge, were hugely successful and formed a connection with viewers. His inclination to integrate strong family dramas with emotional threads into every narrative meant that even a plot centred on murder and mystery would ultimately revolve around the relationships rather than mere sleuthing.

Now, fifty years later, *Uljhan* might not be celebrated as a groundbreaking thriller, but it remains an engaging experience for those who appreciate the storytelling techniques of its time. It encapsulates the spirit of mid-1970s' Bollywood – where commercial success often took precedence over sticking to genre norms, and where narratives were crafted to maximize emotional appeal. This is precisely why Raghunath Jhalani, despite not being a household name, was responsible for creating some of the most memorable films in his lifetime. *Uljhan* may not exemplify a tightly woven mystery, but it triumphs as a family drama infused with thrills and sentimentality.

CAST: Sanjeev Kumar, Sulakshana Pandit, Ashok Kumar, Asrani, Aruna Irani, Farida Jalal, Pinchoo Kapoor, Om Shivpuri
OTHER CREDITS: Directed by Raghunath Jhalani, Gulzar. Music by Kalyanji–Anandji.
RELEASE DATE: 7 November 1975
BOX OFFICE RESULT: Hit
RUNNING TIME: 2 Hours 17 Mins
TRIVIA: Jaya Bhaduri was the initial choice for the heroine's role after her successful pairing with Sanjeev Kumar in Jhalani's earlier film *Anamika*. However, she didn't accept the role due to her upcoming marriage to Amitabh Bachchan.

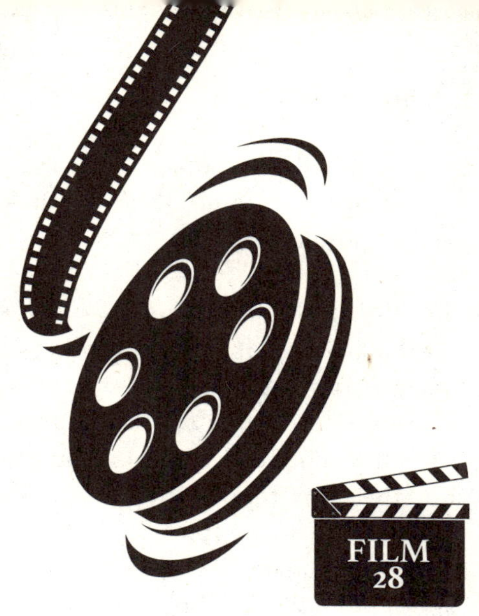

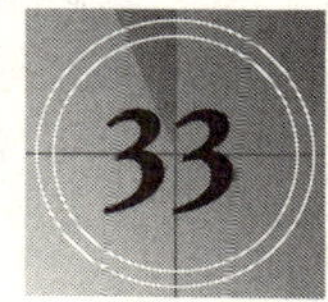

PRAMOD CHAKRAVORTY'S *WARRANT*: AN ACTION CAPER THAT GAVE DEV ANAND'S CAREER A NEW FILLIP

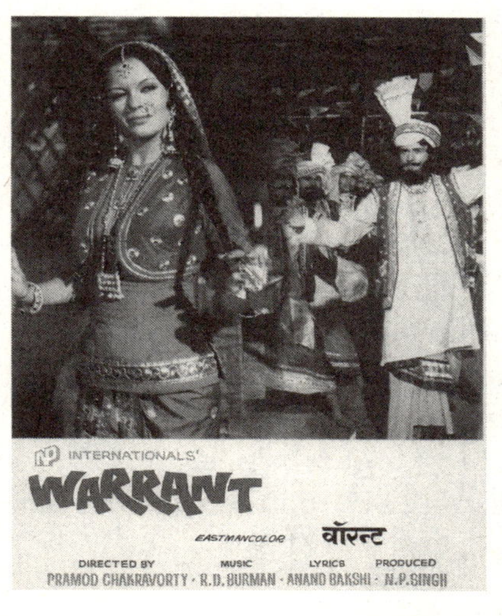

Pramod Chakravorty's *Warrant* is another classic masala blockbuster that brilliantly tapped into the trends of its time. With notable performances by Dev Anand, Zeenat Aman, Pran, Ajit and Satish Kaul, the film was a commercial triumph that solidified Dev Anand's star status in the mid-1970s – a period largely defined by Amitabh Bachchan's angry

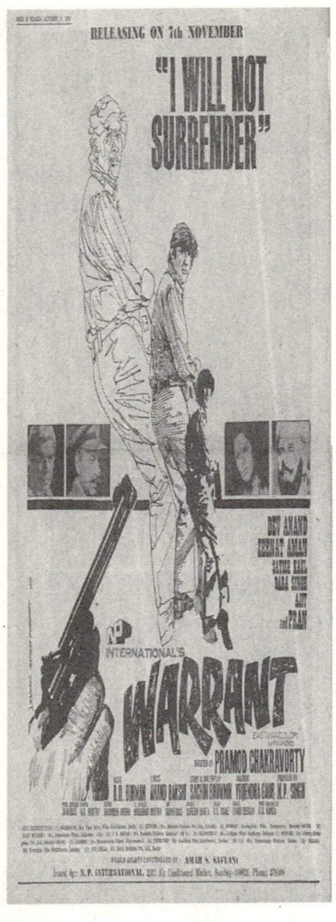

young man image, Rajesh Khanna's romantic allure and Dharmendra's action-hero charisma.

While *Warrant* adheres to the well-worn tropes of that period, its uniqueness as a memorable experience thanks to its polished direction, charismatic performances and the chart-topping music by R.D. Burman. Yet, despite its success and popularity, *Warrant* has its shortcomings. The film's dependence on Hollywood influences, an oft-predictable storyline and a lack of thematic richness mark it as a product of its era rather than a milestone in Bollywood's history. Still its undeniable entertainment factor ensures it remains appealing to audiences.

Essentially, *Warrant* is an adrenaline-fuelled chase film where Jailor Arun Mehra (Dev Anand) facilitates the escape of a death-row inmate, Dinesh (Satish Kaul), igniting a high-tension pursuit involving Arun's father I.G. Mehra (Pran), an unwavering woman named Rita (Zeenat Aman) and a criminal mastermind called Master (Ajit). The movie utilizes a classic cat-and-mouse chase with the protagonist constantly eluding various factions, leading to exhilarating sequences that keep viewers on the edge of their seats.

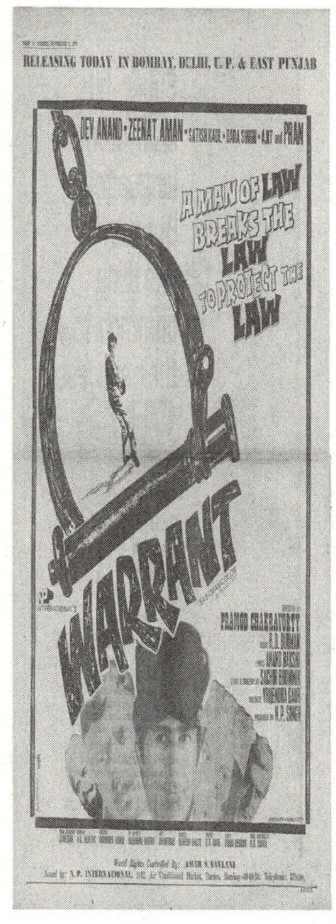

The screenplay is crafted to maximize action and intrigue, ensuring that dull moments are few and far between. However, much like many masala films of that time, logical coherence often takes a back seat to visual spectacle. Characters make abrupt revelations, betrayals occur with little context and plot twists appear mainly to astonish the audience rather than to enhance the narrative. Despite this, the film maintains a brisk pace, fuelled by Pramod Chakravorty's commercial sensibilities and Dev Anand's magnetic screen presence.

By the mid-1970s, Dev Anand was an established veteran, having been a leading figure since the late 1940s. The emergence of newer stars – especially Amitabh Bachchan, with films like *Zanjeer* (1973) and *Deewaar* (1975) – threatened to overshadow the older generation. However, *Warrant* serves as clear evidence of Dev Anand's talent for reinvention and his capacity to remain relevant and bankable.

In contrast to the brooding and morally ambiguous heroes typical of Bachchan's films, Dev Anand's Jailor Arun Mehra is a suave character – charming, stylish and morally sound but cheeky. His delivery of lines combined with his signature head tilts and rapid-fire dialogue adds star power to a character that could easily have been another generic action hero. Although his romantic chemistry with Zeenat Aman doesn't match their electric connection in *Heera Panna* (1973), their on-screen pairing still injects the film with moments of light-hearted romance amidst the action

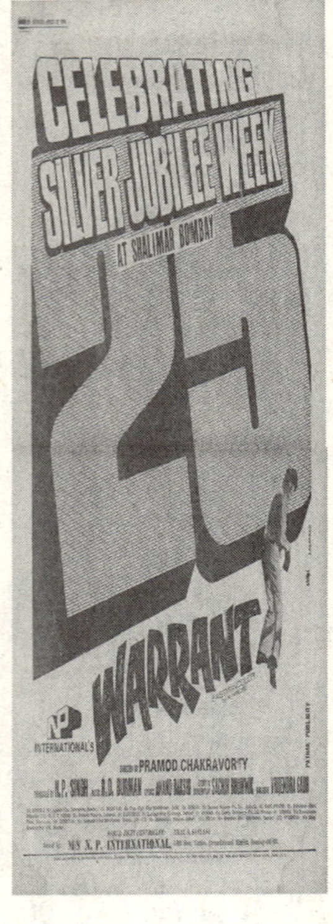

Zeenat Aman's character Rita is intriguing but feels somewhat underdeveloped. Though introduced as a woman on a mission, her motives aren't deeply explored, and she is given little scope beyond serving as a love interest and a narrative catalyst. This reflects a common trend in Bollywood during the time, where even talented actresses were often relegated to secondary roles. Nevertheless, Zeenat's presence and style compensate for some of the script's limitations, and she also radiates confidence and modernity that were a major part of her allure.

Pran, as I.G. Mehra, brings substance to a role that could have otherwise been one-dimensional. His conflict with his son adds a layer of familial drama to the film. Ajit, portraying the underworld kingpin Master, embodies the archetypal villain he became known for playing – stylish, composed and menacing. His lines, delivered with a slow and deliberate cadence, make him a noteworthy antagonist. However, the film doesn't explore his character beyond typical villainy, rendering him a formidable yet predictable adversary.

A standout feature of *Warrant* is its overt borrowing from Hollywood. The helicopter landing scene closely mirrors the one from *You Only Live Twice* (1967), showcasing the film's inclination towards Western action motifs. This tendency isn't surprising, given Pramod Chakravorty's affinity for international action aesthetics. His subsequent film, *Baarood* (1976), continued this trend with inspirations drawn from *Summertime Killer* (1972).

While Bollywood's borrowing from Hollywood has always been a prevalent practice, *Warrant* doesn't effectively weave these inspirations into its storyline in a commendable manner. Instead, these segments come off as flashy spectacles rather than consequential parts of the story, and this lack of originality is among *Warrant's* major weaknesses.

A key strength of the movie is its music composed by R.D. Burman. The soundtrack includes several catchy tracks, with '*Ruk Jaana O Jaana*' being the highlight, skyrocketing to immense popularity. This song, filled with energetic rhythms and Kishore Kumar's spirited vocals, captures the essence of the film – playful yet engaging. Burman's music during the 1970s served as a vital component in many films' triumphs, including *Warrant,* in which the songs are seamlessly interwoven into the plot to a delightful effect.

Five decades later, *Warrant* can still be considered an entertaining watch, primarily due to Dev Anand's star allure and the strong sense of nostalgia it induces. Yet, when assessed critically, the film falls short of the depth and narrative sophistication evident in some of its contemporaries.

In contrast to groundbreaking films released in the same year, such as *Deewaar* and *Sholay*, *Warrant* feels more like a commercial venture than an artistic endeavour. Nevertheless, this is exactly what has made it a cult classic wrapped in a polished, star-studded package.

For Pramod Chakravorty, *Warrant* was a unique collaboration with Dev Anand, yet it solidified that even as Bollywood evolved into a new era dominated by grittier storylines and emerging stars, Dev Anand continued to be a formidable presence.

Warrant may not be a masterpiece, nor does it rank among the greatest films of the 1970s. However, it is still an entertaining film that highlights the timeless charisma of Dev Anand, the star power of Zeenat Aman and the musical genius of R.D. Burman. While its Hollywood inspirations and predictable plot structure limit its groundbreaking potential, its undeniable fun factor ensures it remains a cherished classic among fans of 1970s' Bollywood.

CAST: Dev Anand, Zeenat Aman, Pran, Ajit, Satish Kaul
OTHER CREDITS: Directed by Pramod Chakravorty. Music by R.D. Burman.
RELEASE DATE: 7 November 1975
BOX OFFICE RESULT: Hit
RUNNING TIME: 2 Hours 19 Mins
TRIVIA: Although he played Dev Anand's father in the movie, Pran was only three years older than Dev Anand in real life.

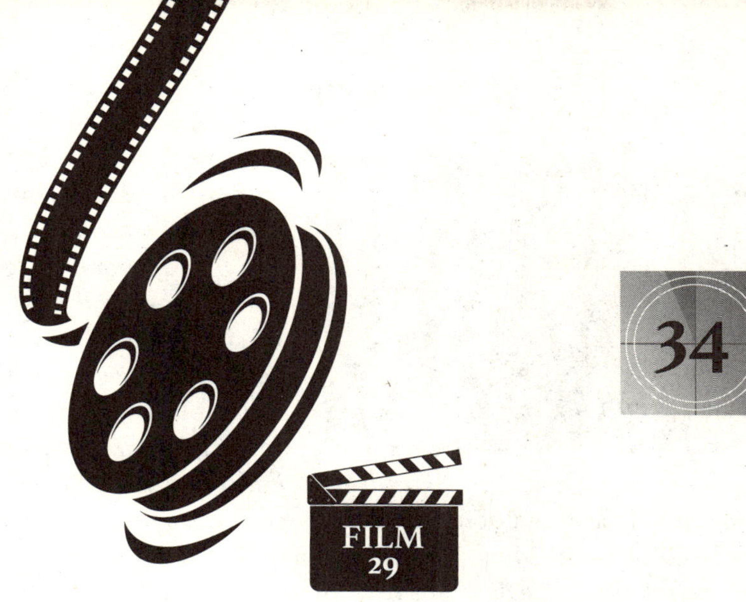

TAHIR HUSSAIN'S *ZAKHMEE*: A COMMERCIAL MIX OF REVENGE, FAMILY DRAMA AND ROMANCE

Tahir Hussain's film *Zakhmee*, released in 1975, stands as a notable example of Bollywood's vibrant masala era, a time when the magnetism of stars and emotional storytelling determined box-office success rather than innovative narratives. While the film presents an intriguing story – a man wrongfully accused of murder, his brothers' desperate quest for justice and an exhilarating prison break – it ultimately stumbles due to a formulaic screenplay and inconsistent execution. Nonetheless, *Zakhmee* found its audience buoyed by the commanding presence of Sunil Dutt, the youthful charm of Reena Roy and a lively soundtrack by the (then) emerging composer Bappi Lahiri.

At its heart, *Zakhmee* explores themes of betrayal, family

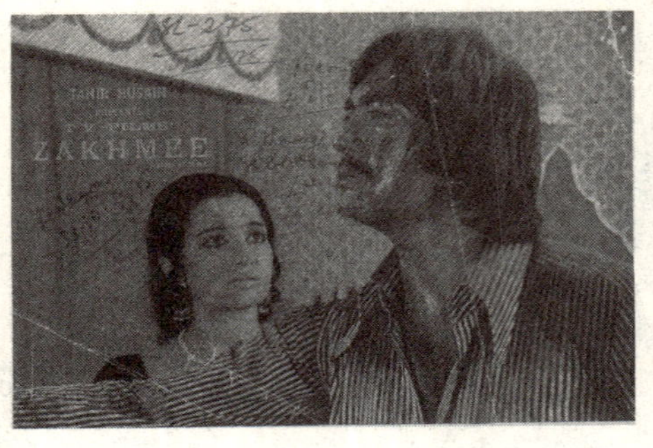

bonding and revenge, typical of films from that time. Sunil Dutt, enjoying a second lease of his career and fresh off successful hits like *Heera* and *Geeta Mera Naam*, plays Anand, an honourable man whose world is shattered when he is unjustly accused of murdering his business partner on the very night of his wedding. This story of a wronged innocent hero who must battle to reclaim his honour was a common thread in Hindi cinema. *Zakhmee* struggles to realize the full emotional and dramatic potential of such a setup. Anand's choice to not outright reject the accusations is captivating but lacks the deep psychological exploration it could have led to. Instead, the storyline rushes through predictable twists, like a misguided kidnapping scheme by Anand's younger brothers, Amar and Pawan, which introduces a clichéd romantic angle rather than genuine conflict.

Director Raja Thakur, whose untimely passing at the young age of fifty-one cut short his career after this film, shows moments in which his storytelling skill is visible but ultimately gets caught up in the pitfalls of a formulaic vision. The screenplay lacks focus and jumps erratically between serious courtroom moments, action sequences and romantic scenes, creating a disjointed viewing experience. For instance, Anand's jailbreak, aided by the initially unhelpful but later understanding Dilawar, unfolds too conveniently, thereby removing any suspense from the sequence. The depiction of stereotypical villains such as Tiger (Imtiaz) and the smuggling overlord (Kamal Kapoor) further reduces the film to a basic revenge story. One can't help but ponder how *Zakhmee* could have transcended its limitations with a tighter, more cohesive script.

Despite these structural issues, the film holds the viewer's attention, mainly thanks to its cast. Sunil Dutt offers a solid performance, imbibing Anand with a flair that the screenplay doesn't quite fully support. His emotional intensity truly shines in scenes where he confronts his unjust imprisonment. Reena Roy, in one of her early roles, demonstrates a strong presence with her charm and glamour. The chemistry between her and Rakesh Roshan, though somewhat predictable, brings rare moments of energy to the film. Roshan, delivering a competent performance, fits the role of the devoted younger brother battling against wrongdoing. Tariq, though likeable, serves merely as the one with youthful energy in the group.

Unfortunately, the film's technical elements leave much to be desired. The art direction feels rushed with sets that appear poorly constructed, reflecting the cost-cutting essence of mid-1970s' commercial cinema. The action scenes also lack any finesse, leaning more on exaggerated brawls rather than skilfully choreographed fights. The pacing drags in the second half, where attempts to escalate tension instead feel stretched and meaningless. A tighter edit could have helped maintain the film's momentum more effectively.

What truly cements *Zakhmee's* nostalgic place in Bollywood is its music. Bappi Lahiri, then on the rise, produced a soundtrack that surpassed the movie itself. The title song, performed during a dramatic escape sequence set against the backdrop of Holi, has become iconic. Tracks like '*Abhi Abhi Thi Dushmani*' and '*Nothing is Impossible*' give off an electrifying energy, while '*Jalta Hai Jiya Mera*' offers a sweet romantic pause. Lahiri's compositions add much-needed excitement into a film that otherwise lacked a definitive character. His success with *Zakhmee* marked him as one of Bollywood's most in-demand music directors, paving the way for the disco era that would soon follow in the next decade.

In retrospect, *Zakhmee* can be appreciated for managing to flourish despite its imperfections by adhering to a commercially successful formula. It serves as a testament to how star power, catchy music and a few standout performances can often outweigh a mediocre screenplay and uninspired direction. Its commercial triumph illustrates the 1970s' audience's taste for emotion-driven and star-centric spectacles.

CAST: Sunil Dutt, Asha Parekh, Reena Roy, Rakesh Roshan, Tariq, Kamal Kapoor, Ifteqar, Yunus Parvez
OTHER CREDITS: Directed by Raja Thakur. Music by Bappi Lahiri.
RELEASE DATE: 28 July 1975
BOX OFFICE RESULT: Super Hit
RUNNING TIME: 2 Hours 25 Mins
TRIVIA: Producer Tahir Hussain (father of Aamir Khan) first signed young composer Bappi Lahiri to score the background music of his 1974 film *Madhosh*, which had music by R.D. Burman. It was with *Zakhmee* that Bappi Lahiri got his first big break, and he made the most of his chance by composing some great music which also became hugely popular.

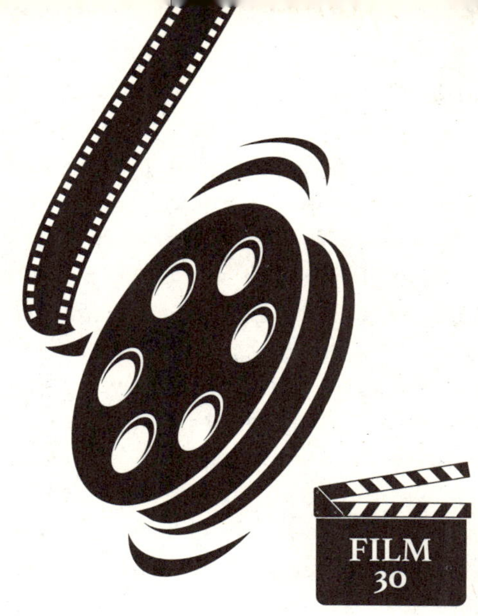

RAVI CHOPRA'S *ZAMEER*: OF MORAL DILEMMAS AND CONFLICT

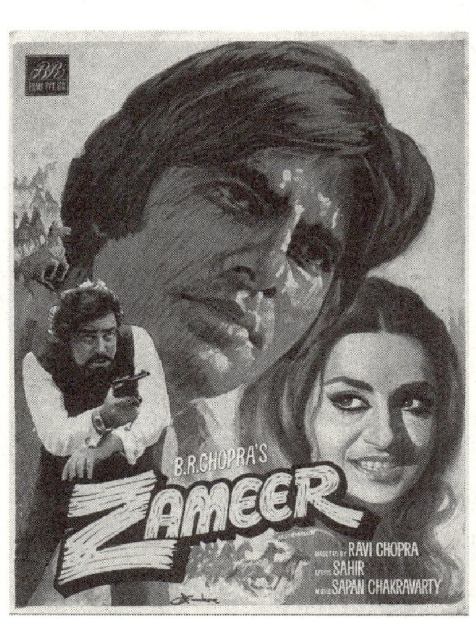

Ravi Chopra's directorial debut, *Zameer*, arrived with a great deal of anticipation due to Ravi being the son of the iconic film-maker B.R. Chopra. The pressure of this legacy meant that his first film was under great scrutiny, prompting him to choose a narrative that had already made the rounds in both Hollywood and Bollywood. *Zameer* drew inspiration from O. Henry's short story

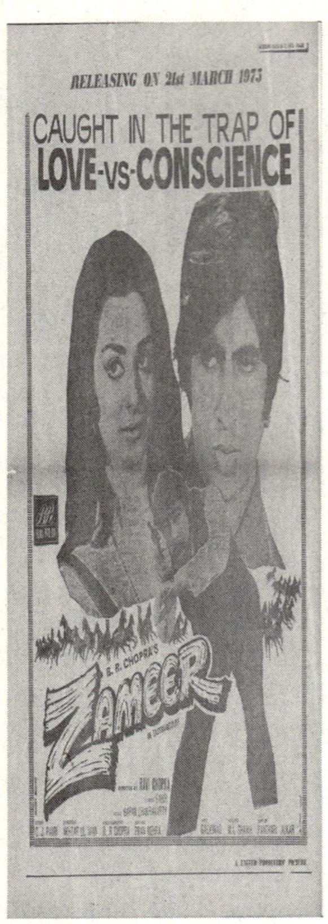

'A Double-Dyed Deceiver', which had previously been transformed into a silent film featuring Jack Pickford in 1920. This same story also heavily influenced Raj Khosla's *Bambai Ka Babu* (1961). As a result, *Zameer* was expected to offer a fresh take on a storyline that was familiar yet complex. The plot centres on a young man who scams his way into a wealthy household by pretending to be their long-lost son. As he gets comfortable in his new life, he unexpectedly falls for his supposed sister (whom he met earlier, before the charade), leading to a moral dilemma. This internal struggle – whether to maintain the facade or come clean – is the core of the film's emotional tension.

Featuring some of the most renowned actors of the era, like Shammi Kapoor, Amitabh Bachchan, Saira Banu, Vinod Khanna, Madan Puri and Indrani Mukherjee, *Zameer* boasted a stellar ensemble cast. However, it was the storytelling and the treatment of the narrative that truly distinguished the film. Tackling such a sensitive topic required a deft touch, and Ravi Chopra skilfully managed to portray the intricacies of relationships, emotional turmoil and psychological tension. The emotional trajectory of the main character was portrayed beautifully, as he wrestled with guilt, love and a longing for redemption. The film's title, *Zameer* (translating to 'conscience'), perfectly echoes this internal battle, as the protagonist finds himself trapped between his past dishonesty and an increasing urge to do the right thing.

At the heart of the film was Amitabh Bachchan, who was just on the brink of superstardom when *Zameer* hit the screens. His performance stood out, with his expressive eyes conveying as much depth as his dialogue delivery. This period marked his evolution from a budding actor to the face of the 'angry young man' trend. His performance in *Zameer* was multi-layered, reflecting his ability to express internal conflict without resorting to unnecessary melodrama. While he would ultimately go on to dominate Bollywood, *Zameer* remains an early testament to his knack for gracefully commanding attention on screen.

Shammi Kapoor and Vinod Khanna played robust supporting roles. Shammi Kapoor, who was famous for his over-the-top roles in the 1960s, began to shift into more character-oriented parts by the mid-1970s, and his role in *Zameer* was an early demonstration of his future career. Vinod Khanna, meanwhile, was emerging as a magnetic leading man, and his performance added balance to the film's tense narrative. He would later partner successfully with Amitabh Bachchan, resulting in numerous blockbuster films. Saira Banu, however, was a somewhat unconventional choice alongside Amitabh Bachchan. Although they eventually co-starred in *Hera Pheri* (1976), their on-screen chemistry never quite developed into a realistic pairing. Her role in *Zameer* felt slightly out of place, lacking the dynamic that could have enhanced their shared moments.

In addition to its excellent performances and engaging storyline, *Zameer* also stood out for its music. Composed by Sapan Chakraborty, a longtime assistant to R.D. Burman, the film's soundtrack was quite successful. The standout track, '*Tum Bhi Chalo Hum Bhi Chalein*', may seem to be just a nod to Frank Sinatra's 'Autumn Leaves' (which was the English version of the French song '*Led Feuillies Mortes*') – it evolved into a timeless tune that continues to be enjoyed by music enthusiasts to date.

Reflecting on the film, *Zameer* deserves accolades for its daring storytelling and nuanced treatment of a morally intricate subject. Ravi Chopra's direction paid off because if its considerable sophistication for a debut film-maker. He successfully showed the public that he had not only inherited his father's storytelling instincts but also infused his own unique viewpoint into the cinematic process. The film grappled with themes of deception, redemption, ethical complexities and the burden of conscience with a level of grace that wasn't always prevalent in mainstream Bollywood (which probably would explain the underwhelming box-office response to this film). *Zameer* is still celebrated for its bold narrative and impactful performances.

CAST: Shammi Kapoor, Amitabh Bachchan, Saira Banu, Vinod Khanna, Madan Puri, Indrani Mukherjee
OTHER CREDITS: Directed by Ravi Chopra. Music by Sapan Chakraborty.
RELEASE DATE: 17 March 1975
BOX OFFICE RESULT: Below Average
RUNNING TIME: 2 Hours 16 Mins
TRIVIA: Saira Banu made her debut playing leading lady opposite Shammi Kapoor in *Junglee* (1961). After another romantic lead with him in *Bluff Master* (1963), she made her third film with Kapoor playing his daughter in *Zameer* (1975).

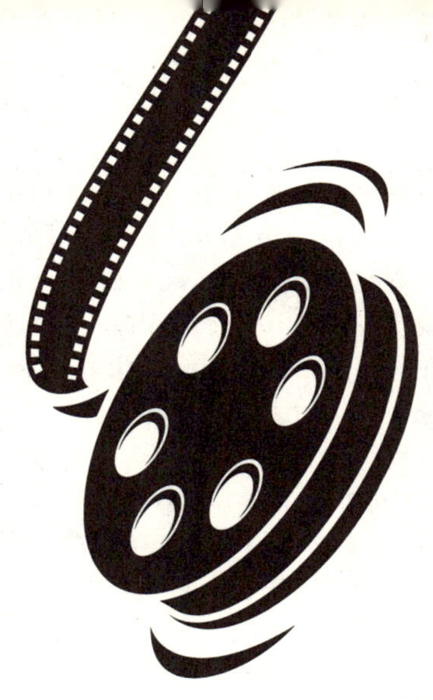

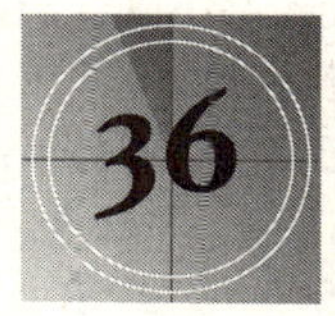

OTHER HINDI FILMS OF 1975

The year 1975 is etched in the annals of Hindi cinema as a watershed moment, largely due to the gigantic impact of films like *Sholay* and *Deewaar*. However, to reduce the cinematic landscape of that year to just its blockbusters would be an injustice to the diverse array of films that found release. Beyond the iconic hits and surprise box office successes, 1975 was a year that reflected the breadth of Bollywood's storytelling, ranging from masala entertainers and melodramas to experimental ventures and cult classics. Many of these films, although not necessarily commercial juggernauts, were notable for reasons other than box office numbers. They showcased genre variety, creative risks and shifting cultural attitudes that added to the richness of commercial Bollywood.

One such example is *Do Thug*, a film that starred Shatrughan Sinha and Hema Malini. Though it was stylistically ahead of its time, resembling the formulaic 1980s masala fare, it struck a chord with audiences and performed well commercially. Hema Malini, who was one of the reigning stars of the time, also delivered a memorable performance in a slightly negative role in *Sunehra Sansar*, a family melodrama directed by A. Subba Rao. Starring alongside Rajendra Kumar and Mala Sinha, Hema's effective portrayal upped the film's emotional quotient. Perhaps more intriguing was the film's musical legacy – it featured a rare collaboration between legendary composer Naushad and Kishore Kumar, culminating in the Kishore Kumar–Asha Bhosle duet '*Hello Hello Kya Haal Hai*'. Oddly, the song was cut from the final version, and Kishore's name was absent from the credits in a puzzling decision that has remained unexplained.

The year also saw Bollywood's tentative flirtations with the superhero genre. *Zorro* starring Navin Nischal and *Toofan* headlined by Vikram, represented unconventional forays into masked vigilante territory. Though not commercially successful, these films remain curiosities in the landscape of 1970s' Bollywood, symbolizing a willingness to experiment with Western themes and ideas and localize them for Indian audiences.

Rishi Kapoor, then a youthful heartthrob, continued to pair successfully with Neetu Singh. After hits like *Khel Khel Mein* and *Rafoo Chakkar*, the duo also appeared together in *Zinda Dil*. Rishi also had a double role in *Raja* opposite Sulakshana Pandit. While these films didn't replicate the commercial success of his earlier releases, Rishi's reputation remained intact due to the momentum gained from his two prior hits.

Rishi's dad Raj Kapoor too had a couple of interesting releases which met with unexpected success. He played an important role in son Randhir's directorial venture and his home production *Dharam Karam*. Raj was also seen as an elderly bumbling detective alongside his friend and *Sangam* co-star Rajendra Kumar in the comic caper *Do Jasoos*. The reasonable success of both films was important to Raj Kapoor, the actor.

The ever-reliable Shashi Kapoor added to the year's cinematic bounty with the classic commercial caper *Salakhein*, while Joginder – known for his kitschy cult classic *Bindiya Aur Bandook* – delivered *Ranga Khush*, a film that catered specifically to his cult fanbase. Joginder's films, while often dismissed by critics, represent a unique subculture within Bollywood, one driven by grassroots popularity and eccentric storytelling.

Dharmendra, enjoying a golden period especially in light of Rajesh Khanna's declining box office pull, had multiple releases including *Saazish* and *Chaitali*, both co-starring Saira Banu. Although delayed, these films managed respectable openings, thanks in no small part to Dharmendra's immense star power. *Ek Mahal Ho Sapno Ka*, another delayed project featuring Dharmendra, had an average box office run buoyed by his charisma.

Randhir Kapoor, who had impressed with his directorial (and acting) venture *Dharam Karam*, featured in two more releases – *Lafange* directed by Harmesh Malhotra and *Ponga Pandit* helmed by Prayag Raj. Notably, *Ponga Pandit* is now seen as the conceptual predecessor to Aditya Chopra's *Rab Ne Bana Di Jodi*, a fascinating example of how thematic DNA can transcend generations in Bollywood storytelling.

Several other films added depth to the year's cinematic output. Basu Bhattacharya's *Tumhara Kalloo*, Sikandar Khanna's *Umar Qaid* and J. Om Prakash's *Aakraman* were all significant for different reasons. *Umar Qaid* especially stood out as a surprise success, illustrating the unpredictable nature of audience preferences.

Another intriguing release of the year was *Aakhri Daao*, directed by A. Salaam and starring Jeetendra and Saira Banu. Based on a novel by Bhagwati Charan Sharma, the film featured a script penned by Salim–Javed, though the writers later distanced themselves from it. That the writers of *Sholay* and *Deewaar* – two of the most defining films of the decade – were also associated with a film like *Aakhri Daao* adds an interesting layer to their 1975 legacy.

In conclusion, while 1975 will forever be celebrated for its landmark films, a deeper and more in-depth exploration reveals a cinematic journey brimming with variety, experimentation and cultural tropes. Whether it was delayed ventures, cult kitsch, experimental genres or overlooked musical gems, the year offered far more than just its headline successes. In terms of sheer diversity and creative output, 1975 was a landmark year that rejuvenated Bollywood's storytelling traditions and provided space to experiment with the evolving tastes of Indian audiences.

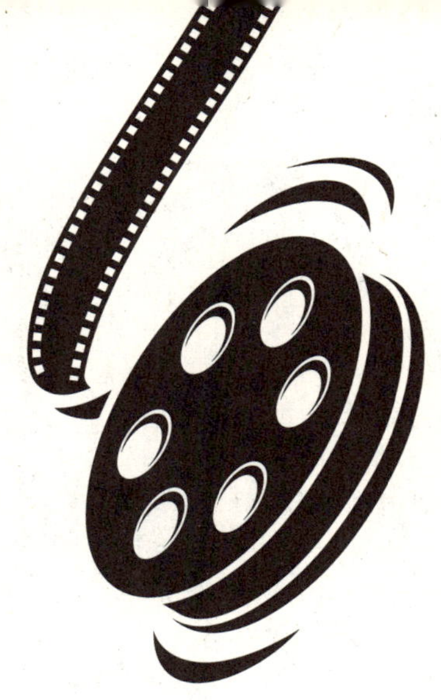

LOST DREAMS: A CHRONICLE OF SHELVED FILMS FROM 1975

The year 1975 was a landmark one in Indian cinema, witnessing the release of iconic films such as *Sholay* and *Deewaar*. However, alongside these blockbusters, the year also saw the unfortunate shelving of several ambitious projects, some of which had the potential to make history. Despite being backed by legendary film-makers, top stars and renowned composers, these films were unable to reach the silver screen, lost forever in the maze of financial troubles, creative roadblocks and other unforeseen circumstances such as ending up in development hell.

DEV ANAND'S UNFULFILLED AMBITIONS

Veteran actor-filmmaker Dev Anand was known for his relentless

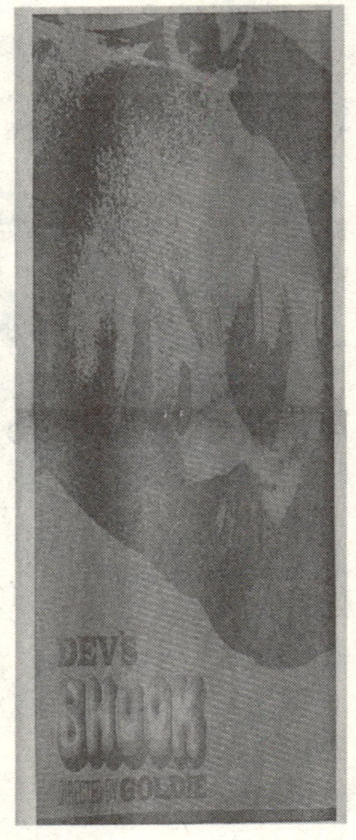

passion for cinema, but not all his dreams materialized. One such project was *Bhook*, which was to be directed by his brother, Vijay Anand, also known as Goldie. Originally announced in 1969, the film was shelved only to be revived in 1975 and then abandoned once again. Vijay Anand, one of the finest film-makers of his time, was known for his craftsmanship, and had *Bhook* been completed, it could have been another feather in his cap.

Another film associated with Dev Anand was *Nawab Aur Sharab* to be directed by Raj Khosla. The film boasted a stellar cast, including Sunil Dutt and Zeenat Aman, yet it never progressed beyond a couple of reels. Khosla and Anand had worked together on successful films before, making the shelving of this project particularly disappointing.

Sawan Kumar Tak's *Mr John* was yet another movie that never saw the light of day. Featuring Dev Anand alongside Rekha, Yogeeta Bali, Tina Munim and Anil Dhawan, the film's announcement was met with great enthusiasm. Usha Khanna was set to compose the music, but the project remained an unfulfilled promise.

THE CURIOUS CASE OF *JWALAMUKHI*

Prakash Mehra, a film-maker known for delivering hits like *Zanjeer*, announced *Jwalamukhi* in November 1975 as a grand multi-starrer featuring Shashi Kapoor, Vinod Khanna, Reena Roy,

Neetu Singh, Asrani, Nirupa Roy and Om Shivpuri. However, the film never materialized in its original form. Mehra later revived it in 1979 with a completely different cast (Shatrughan Sinha, Vinod Mehra, Waheeda Rehman, Shabana Azmi and Raj Babbar), and it was finally released in 1980. Ironically, another film with a similar storyline, *Jyoti Bane Jwala* (Jeetendra), was released just before *Jwalamukhi* and became a super hit. By the time *Jwalamukhi* arrived, audiences had already embraced the other film, leading to its commercial failure.

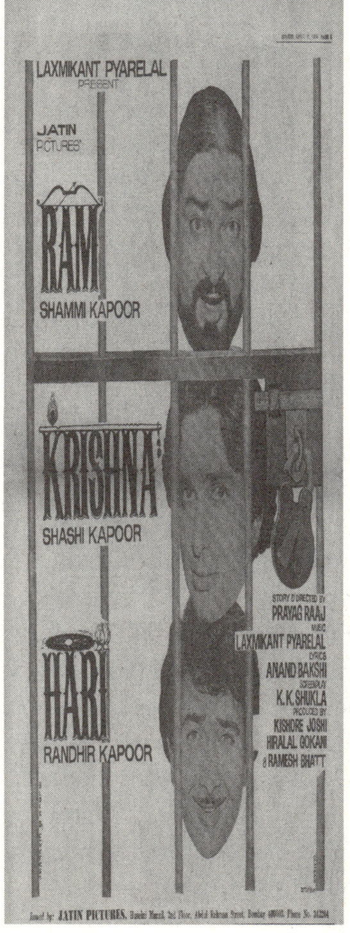

UNREALIZED DREAMS OF LAXMIKANT–PYARELAL

The celebrated music duo Laxmikant–Pyarelal, after years of delivering chart-topping songs, decided to produce their own film, *Ram Krishna Hari*. The project was an exciting venture featuring Shammi Kapoor, Shashi Kapoor and Randhir Kapoor, with a screenplay by Prayag Raj. Despite the promising setup, the film never advanced beyond its announcement stage, leaving fans wondering what might have been.

PEARL PICTURES' SUNKEN SHIP: *SAMANDAR*

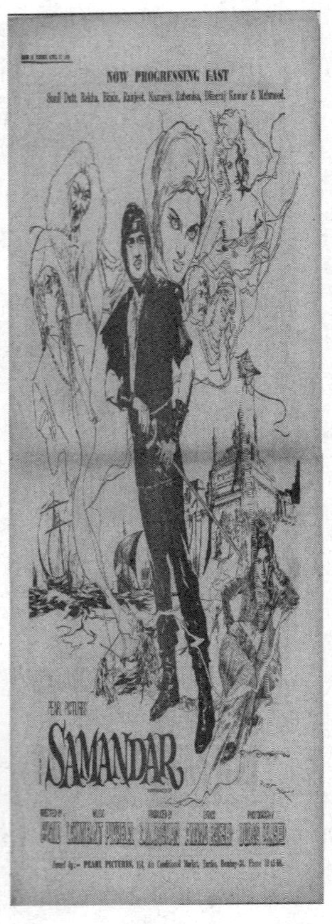

Pearl Pictures had ambitious plans for *Samandar*, which was being directed by Chand. The film starred Sunil Dutt, Rekha, Bindu, Ranjeet, Nazneen and Mehmood and had reportedly completed eleven reels of shooting before it was abandoned. The reasons behind its shelving remain unclear, but its incomplete status is proof of the uncertainties of film-making.

RAJESH KHANNA'S UNFINISHED EPICS

The phenomenon known as Rajesh Khanna was at the peak of his career in the 1970s, yet several of his projects remained incomplete. Among them was *Majnoon*, a magnum opus announced in December 1975 and backed by his father-in-law, Chunibhai Kapadia. The film, directed by the legendary Kamal Amrohi, had an extraordinary ensemble cast, including Raj Kapoor, Shammi Kapoor, Ashok Kumar and Dilip Kumar in a special role, along with Parveen Babi and Simple Kapadia. However, despite its grandeur, the film never progressed beyond a few days of shooting. Khayyam was the music director of the film, and one song was recorded for it, which is available amongst collectors.

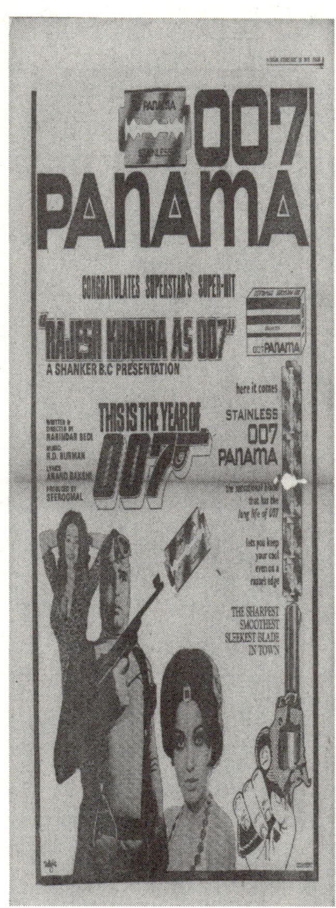

Another intriguing project was *007*, an espionage thriller featuring the superstar in the title role, with Padmini Kapila and Katy Mirza as his leading ladies. Directed by Nagender Bedi with music by R.D. Burman, the film could have been India's answer to James Bond, but it was shelved after only a few days of shooting.

Adding to Khanna's list of unfinished films was an untitled project announced in February 1975 by producer B.K. Gupta. However, nothing concrete materialized from the announcement, leaving another film to join the long list of abandoned ventures.

Although many of these projects had the potential to become classics, they remained unrealized due to a variety of reasons – lack of funding, creative differences or changing market dynamics. While some film-makers attempted to revive their projects, as seen with *Jwalamukhi*, others faded into oblivion.

HINDI FILMS RELEASED IN 1975

	TITLE	CAST	DIRECTOR
1	*Aaja Sanam*	Feroz Khan, Tanuja	Yusuf Naqvi
2	*Aag Aur Toofan*	Robin Kumar, Mumtaz	Tanvir Ahmed
3	*Aakhri Daao*	Jeetendra, Saira Banu, Ranjeet, Danny, Bindu	A. Salaam
4	*Aakraman*	Sanjeev Kumar, Rekha, Rakesh Roshan	J. Om Prakash
5	*Aandhi*	Sanjeev Kumar, Suchitra Sen	Gulzar
6	*Amanush*	Uttam Kumar, Sharmila Tagore	Shakti Samanta
7	*Anari*	Shashi Kapoor, Sharmila Tagore, Moushumi Chat-terjee	Asit Sen
8	*Andolan*	Neetu Singh, Rakesh Pandey	Lekh Tandon
9	*Anokha*	Shatrughan Sinha, Zarina Wahab	Jugal Kishore
10	*Apne Dush-man*	Dharmendra (sp app), Reena Roy	Kaliash Bhandari
11	*Apne Rang Hazaar*	Sanjeev Kumar, Leena Chandavarkar, Danny	Ravi Tandon
12	*Badnaam*	Baldev Khosa, Nazima	Dilip Bose
13	*Baalak Aur Jaanwar*	Baldev Khosa, Mohan Choti, Dulari	Nanabhai Bhatt
14	*Chaitali*	Dharmendra, Saira Banu, Pradeep Kumar, Bindu	Hrishikesh Mukherjee
15	*Charandas Chor*	Smita Patil	Shyam Benegal
17	*Chori Mera Kaam*	Shashi Kapoor, Zeenat Aman, Pran, Ashok Kumar	Brij Sadanah

18	*Chupke Chupke*	Dharmendra, Sharmila Tagore, Amitabh Bachchan, Jaya Bhaduri, Om Prakash	Hrishikesh Mukherjee
19	*Dafa 302*	Randhir Kapoor, Rekha	K Shrivastava
20	*Deewaar*	Shashi Kapoor, Amitabh Bachchan, Parveen Babi, Neetu Singh, Nirupa Roy	Yash Chopra
21	*Dharam Karam*	Raj Kapoor, Randhi Kapoor, Rekha, Premnath	Randhir Kapoor
22	*Dharmatma*	Feroz Khan, Hema Malini, Rekha, Premnath	Feroz Khan
23	*Dhoti Lota Aur Chowpatty*	Mehmood, Helen, Dharmendra (sp app)	Mohan Choti
24	*Do Jasoos*	Raj Kapoor, Rajendra Kumar, Shailendra Singh, Bhavna Bhatt	Naresh Kumar
25	*Do Jhoot*	Vinod Mehra, Moushumi Chatterjee, Pran	Jitu Thakkar
26	*Do Thug*	Shatrughan Sinha, Hema Malini	S.D. Narang
27	*Dulhan*	Jeetendra, Hema Malini	C.V. Rajendran
28	*Ek Mahal Ho Sapno Ka*	Dharmendra, Sharmila Tagore, Leena Chandavarkar, Ashok Kumar	Devendra Goel
29	*Faraar*	Amitabh Bachchan, Sharmila Tagore, Sanjeev Kumar	Shankar Mukherjee
30	*Ganga Ki Kasam*	Anjana, Johnny Walker	B.S. Ranga
31	*Geet Gaata Chal*	Sachin, Sarika	Hiren Nag
32	*Himalay Se Ooncha*	Sunil Dutt, Malika Sarabhai, Ranjeet	B.S. Thapa

33	*Jaan Haazir Hai*	Shakhar Kapur, Prem Kishen, Urmila Bhatt, Vijay Anand	M.N. Rangroo
34	*Jaggu*	Shatrughan Sinha, Leena Chandavarkar	Samir Ganguly
35	*Jai Santoshi Maa*	Anubha Guha, Bharat Bhushan	Vijay Sharma
36	*Julie*	Vikram, Lakshmi, Om Prakash, Utpal Dutt, Nadira	K.S. Setumadhavan
37	*Kaala Sona*	Feroz Khan, Parveen Babi, Danny, Prem Chopra	Ravikant Nagaich
38	*Kagaz Ki Naao*	Raj Kiran, Sarika	B.R. Ishara
39	*Kehte Hain Mujhko Raja*	Dharmendra, Hema Malini, Biswajeet, Rekha, Shatrughan Sinha	Biswajeet
40	*Khel Khel Mein*	Rishi Kapoor, Neetu Singh, Rakesh Roshan, Aruna Irani, Ifteqar	Ravi Tandon
41	*Khushboo*	Jeetendra, Hema Malini	Gulzar
42	*Lafange*	Randhir Kapoor, Mumtaz, Pran	Harmesh Malhotra
43	*Mausam*	Sanjeev Kumar, Sharmila Tagore	Gulzar
44	*Mazaaq*	Vinod Mehra, Moushumi Chatterjee, Mehmood	Haider Ali
45	*Mere Sajna*	Navin Nishchal, Raakhee	Kewal Kumar
46	*Mere Sartaj*	Satish Kaul, Zaheera	Abdul Rashid Kardar
47	*Mili*	Amitabh Bachchan, Jaya Bhaduri, Ashok Kumar, Aruna Irani	Hrishikesh Mukherjee
48	*Naatak*	Vijay Arora, Moushumi Chatterjee, Pran	Sohanlal Kanwar

49	*Neelima*	Vinod Mehra, Zaheeda	Pushparaj
50	*Nishant*	Anant Nag, Shabana Azmi, Smita Patil, Amrish Puri, Naseeruddin Shah	Shyam Benegal
51	*Ponga Pandit*	Randhir Kapoor, Neeta Mehta, Danny	Prayag Raj
52	*Pratiggya*	Dharmendra, Hema Malini, Ajit	Dulal Guha
53	*Prem Kahani*	Rajesh Khanna, Mumtaz, Shashi Kapoor	Raj Khosla
54	*Qaid*	Vinod Khanna, Leena Chandavarkar	Atmaram
55	*Raaja*	Rishi Kapoor, Sulakshana Pandit	K Shankar
56	*Rafoo Chakkar*	Rishi Kapoor, Neetu Singh, Paintal, Rajendranath, Asrani	Narender Bedi
57	*Raftaar*	Vinod Mehra, Moushumi Chatterjee	Dinesh Ramnesh
58	Ranga Khush	Joginder, Dheeraj Kumar, Nazneen, Aruna Irani	Joginder Shelly
59	*Rani Aur Lalpari*	Jeetendra, Rajendra kumar, Reena Roy, Feroz Khan	Ravikant Nagaich
60	*Romeo in Sikkim*	Shyam Kumar, Rajan Haskar, Jr Mehmood	Hari Kishen Kaul
61	*Saazish*	Dharmendra, Saira Banu	Kalidas
62	*Salaakhein*	Shashi Kapoor, Sulakshana Pandit	A .Salaam
63	*Sankalp*	Sulakshana Pandit, Farida Jalal	Ramesh Saigal
64	*Sanyasi*	Manoj Kumar, Hema Malini, Pran, Premnath	Sohanlal Kanwar
65	*Sewak*	Vinod Khanna, Neetu Singh	S.M. Abbas

66	*Sholay*	Dharmendra, Amitbah Bachchan, Sanjeev Kumar, Hema Malini, Jaya Bhaduri, Amjad Khan	Ramesh Sippy
67	*Sunehra Sansar*	Rajendra Kumar, Mala Sinha, Hema Malini	A. Subba Rao
68	*Toofan*	Vikjram, Priyadarshini	Kedar Kapoor
69	*Toofan Aur Bijle*	Arvind Kumar, Zaheera, Imtiaz, Randhwa	Homi Wadia
70	*Tumhara Kalloo*	Kuldeep Baghi, Kajri, Bharat Bhushan	Basu Bhattacharya
71	*Uljhan*	Sanjeev Kumar, Sulak-shana Pandit,	Raghunat Jhalani
72	*Umar Qaid*	Sunil Dutte, Reena Roy, Jeetendra, Vinod Mehra	Sikander Khanna
73	*Vandana*	Parikshit Sahni, Sadhna, Sarika	Narendra Suri
74	*Vardaan*	Vinod Mehra, Reena Roy, Mehmood, Om Prakash, Narendranath	Arun Bhatt
75	*Warrant*	Dev Anand, Zeenat Aman, Pran, Ajit	Pramod Chakaborty
76	*Zakhmee*	Sunil Dutt, Asha Parekh, Rakesh Roshan, Reena Roy, Tariq	Raja Thakur
77	*Zameer*	Shammi Kapoor, Amitabh Bachchan, Vinod Khanna, Saira Banu	Ravi Chopra
78	*Zinda Dil*	Rishi Kapoor, Neetu Singh,Pran	Sikander Khanna
79	*Zindagi Aur Toofan*	Sajid Khan, Yogita Bali	Umesh Mathur
80	*Zorro*	Navin Nischal, Rekha	Shibu Mitra

ACKNOWLEDGEMENTS

Ma Baba for all your love, blessings and encouragement.
Mamma for all your love and support.
Parveez Prabodh and Amrita for being my rocks-forever.
Bhavesh Bhimani for being the starting point for this book
Ashok Kumar for all the support anytime all the time.
Sanjay Mishra, Sudarshan Talwar, Ranjeet Kumar, Saikat Dutta for valuable information, photographs etc.
Sunipa Bhattacharya for always encouraging me to write this book.
Bijit Banerjee and Shashi Rao for all things Pancham and Hindi cinema.
Deepa Buty, Hoshang Bhamgara, Divya Solgama, Manish Mehrotra, Abhishek Khare, Ayushman Mitra for being my reference guides to all things cinema. I keep learning more about cinema every day from all of you.
Mousumi Sengupta, Atri Bhattacharya for being a strong support in ways even you don't know.
Thomas Abraham, Anirban Sarkar and Team Hachette for all the support.
Eunice D'Souza for making me fall in love with literature.